PUBLIC PERSONS and PRIVATE LIVES

PUBLIC PERSONS and PRIVATE LIVES

Intimate Interviews

Cal Thomas

WORD BOOKS
PUBLISHER

For

RAY

with loving gratitude for willingly
walking beside me during my times in the
valley of discouragement, and for

OUR LORD

Who walks between us

Contents

Contents

Preface

In my opinion, Dr. Francis Schaeffer is the greatest living philosopher-theologian in the world today. He has had an enormous influence on my spiritual and intellectual life, and he has taught me that one does not have to hang one's brain on a hook and take a leap of faith in the dark to become a Christian.

I have always regarded Dr. Schaeffer as a man far above me and, although I know him and love him as a brother in Christ, I have viewed him from a distance as one whom I could respect but with whom I could hardly ever expect to identify at any level.

Then, on a visit to Houston, Texas, where we used to live, Dr. Schaeffer shared with my wife, Ray, that he is a manic depressive who must fight depression every day of his life! At that moment I could identify with Dr. Schaeffer as a fellow sinner saved by grace—a man who is susceptible, as I am, to the consequences of living in a fallen world.

That experience caused me to start thinking about what has resulted in this book.

We have all had times on the mount, when we have seen things from God's standpoint and have wanted to stay there; but God will never allow us to stay there. The test of our spiritual life is the power to descend; if we have power to rise only, something is wrong. It is a great thing to be on the mount with God, but a man only gets there in order that afterwards he may get down among the devil-possessed and lift them up. . . . We are built for the valley, for the ordinary stuff we are in, and that is where we have to prove our mettle.

—Oswald Chambers in
My Utmost for His
Highest, October 1

Introduction

There is a common belief among most lay Christians that their well-known brothers and sisters—the evangelical superstars—have their lives together and are always "walking on mountain tops" with God. In part, this belief stems from the prominence of their positions, the books they write telling of overwhelming victories, the image they project on television or in public speaking engagements—or our limited opportunities to view these people in situations that are not controlled.

My colleague, Forrest Boyd, overheard a religious broadcaster who had just viewed a pilot television soap opera with a Christian perspective. Forrest said the man was "tsk-tsking" that the soap opera should not be shown on TV because it portrayed Christians as persons who sometimes have problems. Heaven forbid!

But when we are honest about it, don't we really believe that these Christian superstars are as close to perfect as it is possible to get on this earth? And when we feel that way about them, how do we then feel about ourselves? Guilty? We say, "Oh, if only I could have the faith of a Billy Graham or the power of a president or the influence of so-and-so."

How would you feel if you knew that these leaders sometimes fight with their wives or husbands, that they sometimes have doubts about themselves and even about God, that they become depressed, worry about the future, feel unloved? Far from adversely reflecting on the Christian life, I believe such knowledge about these "pillars of the church" would serve to encourage other Christians (and nonbelievers, too, for that matter) that when we are born again it is not the end, but the beginning.

I think my friend, Wes Pippert, UPI White House Correspondent, put it best when I asked him why he sometimes snaps at people who annoy him. "Because I'm a sinner," said Wes.

God is no respecter of persons and it makes no difference to him how many books a person writes, how many people he preaches to, who is president of a country. He loves us all equally and has a unique plan for each of our lives.

So, far from being above it all, the people you'll read about on these pages are not above temptation, nor do they spend all their time on mountain tops. They are, perhaps, more tempted and more the targets of Satan's attacks than the less well known.

Wesley G. Pippert

White House Correspondent
United Press International

Best wishes & thanks to Wes Pippert

Jimmy Carter 1-18-79

Top: Jimmy Carter meets informally with the press
Below: Wes Pippert presents a copy of *The Spiritual Journey of Jimmy Carter* to the President.

Wes Pippert covers Jimmy Carter's White House for the United Press International wire service. He is the compiler of the recently published book, *The Spiritual Journey of Jimmy Carter: In His Own Words* (MacMillan, 1979).

I first became aware of Wes by reading his byline on the Watergate stories and then, later, through his writings in various Christian periodicals.

In 1974, while my wife and I waited for a plane at Dulles Airport in Washington to take us to Europe for a vacation, my doctor and friend, John Curry and his wife Betsy, showed up and gave us a going-away present. It was a small paperback titled *Memo for '76.* The author was Wes Pippert.

As I read the book, I was impressed by Wes's call for moral considerations to be taken into account in selecting 1976 presidential candidates. The unwritten law among Washington correspondents had been to ignore what candidates did in private so long as he or she showed up for work on time and kept their hands out of the public till. That is finally beginning to change as it has been demonstrated that the moral code a person lives by in private sooner or later must spill over into the public arena.

I was also impressed by Wes's Christian commitment and I wondered to myself how effective a Christian could be at the exalted level of a White House correspondent.

We exchanged letters from time to time as fellow reporters and fellow Christians. However, since I worked at a television station in Houston, I never met Wes until October, 1976, on Jimmy Carter's "Peanut One" airplane flying between Houston and Dallas. We were surprised to see each other and he asked me about Carter's chances in Texas. Then it was time for my private interview with the president-to-be and that was it, until I returned to Washington in the late spring of 1977.

But I liked Wes Pippert and I wanted him to be among the first people interviewed for this book. We met for lunch at a restaurant next door to the famous (and expensive) "Sans Souci." It was "Nick and Dottie's Black Steer." I said we'd eat at the "Sans Souci" as soon as I had a best seller!

Q. *As a Christian, do you find it easier to cover the White House under Carter than you did with Nixon?*

A. Well, previous to Carter I covered the White House only under Ford, for about four months. During the Nixon years I covered Watergate. I think in both areas, Watergate and Carter, my being a Christian has been of tremendous benefit, not because I'm a better reporter or more aggressive or brighter, because none of that would be true.

I think the key to understanding Carter is the fact that he is a Christian. I don't want to be presumptuous about it but I think I understand what that means more than most reporters. On Watergate, the cause of Watergate was really a moral one—and the real story of Watergate was not the break-ins and tapes. The real story of Watergate was power and how it corrupted and how people who had it were so vulnerable to abusing it. Those are ideas that a Christian would understand more than a non-Christian.

Q. *So many people are still saying that Carter is an enigma. Do you think this is directly related to their own lack of spirituality, that those who perhaps don't have much spiritual depth view him as an enigma?*

A. I think so. I think reporters in this town (and reporters are good in this town), look at Carter much as they'd look at any other politician. They tend to look at him in terms of how effective he is—how effective he is on Capitol Hill, how effective he is internationally. I try to look at those things, too, but I also try to look at him in a way that others may not and that is, What is the core of the man? What's his basic motivation? I think the fact that he's a Christian explains a lot . . . who he is and what he does. For one thing, it explains the austerity of his life style.

Just before I came over (to lunch) I was talking on the telephone to Phil Drysdale of the Op-Ed page of the *New York Times.* I said to him, "You take the Middle East and speak of boundaries, of Palestinian refugees . . . Carter outside the Baptist Church that morning when Sadat visited Jerusalem . . . Carter, Begin, and Sadat all spoke of the Middle East in religious terms. They said we serve and worship the same God." That presents an interesting situation I'd really never thought about before. You see, Arabs will tell you that the Moslems look to Abraham as we all look to Abraham. I don't know. I've had to do a lot of thinking about that. Is their God really the God of Abraham? They would say that he is. So, in some ways at least, all three men look at the Middle East in religious terms. We look at it in political terms.

Q. *Going back to what you said earlier about your being able to understand Carter because you, also, are a Christian. Does that understanding color your objectivity about him? Does it mean you have empathy for him, that you have personal feelings?*

A. I love Jimmy Carter. I think that anyone who talks to me knows that. I'm not close to him. There's no relationship whatsoever between us. He does have a relationship with some reporters but he certainly doesn't with me. The fact that I'm a Christian has had nothing to do with any kind of special rapport, has not resulted in any intimacy. But I am very fond of him.

I would also like to point out that the record will show I was the reporter who dug up the stuff on his finances in Plains in December, 1976, a story which angered his staff. I was the one, I think more than any other reporter, who questioned his treatment of minorities. I did it during the campaign—and during the transition. And on two or three occasions I've asked questions at news conferences concerning minorities and Africa. No one else has. I'm the one who asked Carter the first question about Bert Lance. By doing so I flew in the face of ground rules set down at the news conference on welfare (in Plains, Georgia). Yes, I asked him about Bert Lance—and Bert Lance is a friend of mine! And so even though I am very fond of President Carter, I think the record will show I haven't let that get in the way of being tough on him.

Q. *Do you think that might be the reason why intimacy hasn't developed between you and the president, and would you like to see a close relationship develop?*

A. Oh, humanly, certainly I'd like to be close to the president. Who wouldn't? And I wouldn't believe anyone who said he or she didn't want to be so. But professionally, it doesn't matter. I don't care.

Q. *But can you divide yourself that way? Can you categorize yourself into times when you're a professional and times when you're human, so to speak?*

A. Well, that's a judgment you'll have to make—as to whether I'm integrated or not. But I've thought about that aspect of the Christian life more than any other thing in the last three or four years. So what I profess privately and what I believe privately is demonstrated in what I do professionally and publicly. I've really wrestled with that. What does it mean to be a reporter who is a Christian?

Q. *What does it mean?*

A. It doesn't mean that I'm better or smarter than others. Nor does it mean that I'm more aggressive. It doesn't mean that I'll have the inside track with other Christians who are sources. I think it does mean that I try to use and exercise the gifts God has given me through his Holy Spirit. And I must try to use those gifts to the glory of God. It may be that along the way because I am a Christian my conscience and my perception of things have been sharpened—and it may mean I perceive things that others don't. Whether I'm able to follow through on it or not is something else again. But understanding the spiritual dimension of President Carter is important to understanding him. It is also important to perceive the spiritual problems that resulted in Watergate. I did not win any prizes on Watergate, but I understood Watergate.

Q. *Does the cynicism and sometimes open hostility toward Carter's faith ever bother you?*

A. I don't know. I've been around cynicism a long time. I might point out, though, what Jody Powell told me during an interview in '76. At the end of the interview I asked him how he felt the media had handled the moral dimension of Carter's life, and he replied, "I think the American people have a far better understanding of Carter's life than do the people charged with communicating it. They've either been biased or slip-shod and bizarre in their stories to the extreme because of their disfavor with religious faith." And I believe that. So I guess I'm used to it.

Q. *How do you witness to your colleagues? Do you ever refrain from sharing your faith because you're in the minority? I think someone took a survey which showed that out of a couple of thousand or more reporters accredited to report the news from Washington, only a dozen or so said they were evangelical Christians. Do you have opportunities to witness? Do you feel the White House is your mission field?*

A. I really hope that I'm a whole person and that there's not one part of my life devoted to my job and another part devoted to witnessing to colleagues. I don't want this answer to be a copout on being verbal, but I think the best witness is a total life. That includes relationships and it includes conversation—and it includes a certain excellence in the way you approach what you do. I hope that when there are opportunities to be vocal I don't shun them.

Q. *Can you give me an example as to when you might have had such an opportunity? For instance, it's no secret that on some presidential trips there's a lot of partying, heavy drinking, and some fooling around. Do you have opportunities to speak to that?*

A. I'm not sure I would tell a person that he shouldn't be sleeping around. I don't think so. Such an action may be trying to impose Christian behavior on non-Christians. I wonder how productive it is. I wonder if we can expect people who are not Christians to live by Christian standards.

Last night I led a Bible study in Georgetown and will do the same thing tonight on John 4. Jesus had that conversation with the woman at the well. The first thing he did was to get acquainted with the stranger. He asked her for a drink and he talked with her. It wasn't until further in the conversation that he got around to witnessing to her.

Even if we use Christ's pattern, the way to witness is to first of all be a whole person and relate to the other person. There have been times when I haven't been as vocal as I should . . . but I know that, nonetheless, I am identified in the press corps as a Christian.

Q. *Do they ever give you any flak for that? Are you the butt of any jokes or are you respected?*

A. I don't know. I think I'm respected. I hope so. But I did have conversations of some significance in Plains, sometimes late at night when I'd sit around and talk, one on one. And in my bureau, there are times when I have meaningful conversation. At least we talk about basic matters. This whole concept is troublesome. It's something that I'm still wrestling with. How serious should you be vocally?

Q. *On the occasions when you do have time for in-depth conversations with your fellow reporters, do you ever get beyond the basic stereotypes of what it means to be a Christian: don't drink, don't smoke, don't chew, don't go with girls who do?*

A. I try not to talk about such things as liquor and cigarettes. I think the Bible says something about liquor. Not much, though. It's totally silent on smoking. But I think in dealing with people, it gets down to six basic questions as to whether a person has found fulfillment and joy in living. And as near as I can tell there are few non-Christians who have found fulfillment and joy in living. They acknowledge that they haven't. And are they satisfied with their personal relationships? I've found very few people in conversations who are satisfied with their personal relationships.

The thing in this town (Washington, D.C.) is that marriages are falling apart. There are family problems, marital difficulties. I'm single so I can't really counsel and don't counsel in these marital situations. But they indicate a real hunger for something. Just the tragedies of common living, the problems of a job, the boss— those things are really profound. To talk about whether a person drinks or not is really pretty superficial compared to those kinds of questions. I think that's where Scripture and an experience with Christ can provide some help, some answers.

You know, in John 4 where Jesus was having a conversation with the woman—he didn't talk about liquor. He spoke about relationships. One of the most meaningful conversations I've had was with a fellow whose marriage was in trouble. He was then contemplating separation and has since separated. Another conversation was with a fellow whose marriage was intact but who had serious problems involving a daughter. I had another conversation with a fellow who had no emotional problems, but he had a curiosity about Carter . . . Carter's beliefs. His curiosity about Carter led into a discussion about spiritual matters.

Q. *Do you think some of these people come to you or search you out because you have your act together or are these just happenstance meetings?*

A. I don't know if anything ever occurs as the result of happenstance. God brings people into our lives at necessary times. I don't think I'm sought out. That bothered me a great deal during university days. I'd been a Christian for a long time prior to that and I became involved with Inter-Varsity on campus in Iowa. I've also talked to Becky about this (Wes' fiancée). Becky's something else. She's animated and dynamic. She can be traveling on an airliner or a bus and within half an hour . . . she knows no strangers.

But she moves around a lot on the campuses and talks about evangelism. I don't mean this frivolously, but why is she effective? Because her parents raised her to be very outgoing? If that's the case then it's just a matter of having a pleasing personality to be a good witness. That concept really intimidated me when I was in college. Obviously there are Christians who are not sought out and I don't think those Christians should feel in any way inferior.

Q. *Everyone has an Achilles heel. Everyone has an area that Satan attacks. Are you ever tempted to compromise on a story?*

A. The problems I face in life are not professional, they are personal. And I think they deal with the way I view people—well, not the way *I* view *them;* I think my view of them is good. But I sometimes think the way it works out is something less than it ought to be. I can be abrasive, not so much in my professional relationships, but in my personal relationships. I can't justify that, not in any way can I justify that.

Q. *Abrasive—how?*

A. Oh, like in cutting. I can be devastating.

Q. *Why do you do that?*

A. Because I'm a sinner. In spite of my abrasiveness, however, my family relationship is good, really good. I have a tightly knit family. The best man I know, the man I'd rather be with more than any other man in the world is my brother, who's a farmer. The person I'd rather talk to than anyone else is my sister.

Q. *Are you the oldest?*

A. No, I'm the fifth out of seven.

Q. *How old are you?*

A. Forty-two. My mother is spiritually powerful and a re-markable woman in her own right. She's 82 and lives alone on the farm. So my family relationships are very solid and the close relationships that I've had have been good. I don't have too many regrets. One of the prob-lems, though, having said that, is the peripheral rela-tionships. You know, the guy who's at the desk in my apartment building. He doesn't answer the phone when he's supposed to.

I deposited a check this morning and the woman asked me, "What's that for?" It was an honorarium I had received from a college and she wanted to know what it was for. And my first reaction was "What busi-ness is that of yours?" I said something like "Why do you want to know? I've been banking here for ten years." She said, "I'm new here and I just need to know." I said, "It's not for reporting. I'm a reporter. It's an hono-rarium. I do some speaking." I had no reason to be tart with her. I can't justify that. She didn't know who I was but the fact that I was anonymous didn't justify what I was doing.

And I wear a belt with a big buckle so that every time I go through the line (at airports) it touches off the machine and the last couple of times they made me take it off and I fired back at them—and how do I justify that? How do I justify my driving habits? Those are superficial.

I'm single. I've always been single. And it wasn't the close relationships I had (with women) that provided the problems. It was the relationships I had on a casual basis. I don't mean I always treated those casual rela-tionships with Christian integrity. I know I didn't. I

do a lot of things and I'm generally in a hurry going
here and there. People will stop me and want to talk.
Now nothing just happens. God brings people into your
life. Well, if a person wants to talk and my only concern
is to hurry so I can take off and do something else, I
may well be turning my back on a need which that
person has.

Q. *Talking about weaknesses, how much of a problem is
the ego factor for you? You're a White House Correspondent which is the ultimate, for many, if not all the press.
Is that a problem for you, if not of attainment, since
you have attained, then perhaps of preservation?*

A. People say it doesn't appear to be a problem for me,
but humility is so light a grace, the moment you think
you have it, you've lost it. So I look at myself as honestly
as I can. I'm very proud of my job. It's heady stuff. I
think of my inner core and I'm extremely proud. I don't
like embarrassment. But I try to guard against seeing
my job as something it is not.

I've used this example a couple of times. Some months
ago, Gromyko (the Soviet Foreign Minister) was at the
White House. He came outside after it was over. He
stood and we interviewed him for a few minutes. As
I stood only ten feet away from him, I thought, *Isn't
this amazing? Here is a man who probably knows more
secrets about the Soviet Union over the last 25 years
that he's been foreign minister than anyone else.* And
he talked a bit. But I thought, *I might as well be on
the moon as far as knowing what is going on inside his
head.* Proximity physically is not to be confused with
intimacy. I see Carter two or three times a day for

photo opportunities or one thing or another, but that is not to be confused with being intimate with Carter. I'm not. Sometimes the danger is the fact that we correspondents are working at the White House and we're close to where decisions are being made, physically speaking. Some think that makes us intimate with Carter. The two are not the same.

I have a friend who's an organist at a church. She is sometimes awestruck at what I do and I have said, "When you play music this Sunday morning, you are touching more people in more intimate ways than I will in a month's time."

The fact that I cover Carter does not mean that I am intimate with him. I know that one of the problems with Watergate was that the White House press corps became too proud, too fat, too smug, and they missed the story that was right underneath their noses.

Q. *Do you think Watergate might have been exposed a lot earlier or, if not Watergate, at least the abuses of power, if they'd not been that way?*

A. Look. We take a trip, our bags are put on the press plane. The next time we see them, they'll be delivered to our hotel rooms. We don't have to check in. We step off the plane, and we don't need to go through a line. We step directly on to a bus. There's always food there . . . all these little things that other people have to do . . . fight the crowds, fight the baggage, fight the lines at hotels . . . those are all taken care of for us. And if any of these goes awry, we really get upset about it. So do I. And yet that goes toward creating the false image, a false sense of intimacy or importance on the part of reporters. You just have to guard against it.

Q. *You are junior in terms of seniority. You're not the top UPI White House Correspondent. Helen Thomas is. There are a thousand, perhaps millions of workers who are just behind someone else. They feel they can do a better job than the person who is ahead of them and they wonder why they're not on top, why they're not getting the breaks they think they deserve. Is that ever a problem for you?*

A. Well, several things. First, I'm the senior wire service correspondent covering Jimmy Carter. Here's the pride that I was just denying a few minutes ago! No wire service reporter has covered Carter longer than I have. I'm the dean, not of the White House, but in terms of covering Carter. But Helen Thomas has one of the biggest hearts of anyone I know.

A fellow I know works for the telephone company. He travels with the presidential party when the president goes out of town. One time they were in a little town overnight and this man had hired a couple of local women to come in overnight and punch the teletype machines. President Ford and his wife came down and the two women kind of stood up against the wall, intimidated. Helen saw them and went over to them. She led them out to the middle of the floor and introduced them to the Fords. The man said they have never forgotten that. Helen's that way. She cannot tolerate arrogance. But she's a softy when it comes to ordinary people who are having a tough time. She really is. We have, I think, a great relationship.

There are three of us in the bureau. Each of our gifts is different, so I don't think we're in competition. In fact, I was curious that you even talked about that because the other day Larry McQuillan, the third person in the bureau, and I were having lunch and we were talking about it. It was his observation . . . someone else had asked him about competition . . . and he said, "I think all three of us are different and there's no need for us to compete because we have different kinds of interests and skills."

Helen has tremendous contacts all over the White House and she really likes working on a breaking story. I prefer to proceed out of interviews or work on issues now and then, to look at the spiritual aspects of Carter which do not interest her. I don't think she feels as strongly as I do that the spiritual dimension is the key to Carter. And Larry has other skills. He's a good writer. So, together there's no competition. Rather, we complement each other.

Q. *Do you ever have to grapple with feelings of inadequacy, of failure, of loneliness? And if you do, how do you deal with it? One wouldn't expect that a person covering the White House could be lonely . . . all that excitement, standing face to face with the President.*

A. Loneliness has nothing to do with how many people you have around you. Loneliness is a state of mind and soul. To feel lonely, it doesn't matter where you are. I think the same thing is true of inadequacy. Sure I sometimes feel lonely and inadequate, but not neurotically. All this reminds me of when I was growing up . . . I grew up on a farm . . . my father was a tenant farmer most of his life.

Q. *Where was that?*

A. Near Mason City, Iowa. I was afraid of most things—

afraid of the world—afraid of not getting good grades. I was afraid of girls, of meeting new people. But I realized that if I went through life totally inhibited by my fears, I would cut myself off from all kinds of opportunities. For example, I know people in this town who will not apply for a fellowship because they think they might not win and they're not prepared to handle a "no" or "you've lost, you've been rejected." Anyway, I decided I would simply acknowledge the fears, not deny them. I don't think that would have been healthy.

So I didn't say, "I'm not afraid." I said, "I *am* afraid, but I'm going to do it anyway." I acknowledged the fears and went ahead and did it anyway.

I heard that idea expressed at the Kennedy Center two or three years ago in Shakespeare's "Measure for Measure" when Lucio says at one point (he said it negatively, but it makes the point), "Our doubts are traitors and make us lose the good we oft might win by fearing to attempt." So, as a result, I rarely say "no." If someone asks me to do something I say "yes." Now there comes a time when that has to be corrected as well and I'm discovering it right now. All of a sudden I'm overcommitted in my church and I'm going to have to say "no" to some things because you can't do everything and do everything well. Yes, I do feel inadequate but I'm not inhibited by it. Because I am a Christian, I find my inadequacies buttressed by my faith in Christ. In that light I can live my faith.

Arthur S. DeMoss

Insurance Executive

Art DeMoss

"Hardly anyone, including myself, has dealt with it [wealth] very well. At least no one has all the answers," says Art DeMoss, President of National Liberty Corporation of Valley Forge, Pennsylvania, the country's largest mail order insurance company.

Not only is he a millionaire many times over, his background and the story of how he came into money and into the kingdom of God is fascinating.

Art DeMoss was born 52 years ago in Albany, New York. While most kids who would go astray might fall into alcohol or drugs or crime, not Art DeMoss. He was different. He became hooked on gambling!

"It started," he says, "very innocently, with cards that were lying around the house when I was in my early teens. First it was for fun, then for money and a little more money and a little more money. One thing led to another. I began betting on anything: horses, dice, roulette, baseball, and football, just anything. Then, I realized that everyone who gambles, loses, so I decided to get on the other side of the fence and start taking their bets. I started booking horses in my late teens. That just destroyed whatever sense of values I may have had at the time. I don't remember whether I had a set of values or not. Handling a lot of money while I was very young, thousands of dollars a day, making it, losing it—helped prepare me for something better in the future."

Continues DeMoss, "At the time of my conversion I had already gone into the insurance business. I was still gambling heavily but I was not doing it for a living! When I first started (selling insurance) I made more money playing cards than I did writing policies. But after I got converted I found something better and lost interest in gambling."

Much of Art DeMoss's life since his conversion has been taken up by serving others with his time and his money. DeMoss flew to California shortly after the return of former Black Panther leader Eldridge Cleaver and personally discipled him in his new found faith.

He also is responsible for bringing speakers to St. Joseph's in the Hills Catholic Retreat Center in Malvern, Pennsylvania (DeMoss is not Catholic) to deliver evangelistic messages to 400 Catholic men, many of whom subsequently pray for the first time to invite Christ into their lives.

DeMoss is one of those remarkable men who seems untouched and uncorrupted by his vast wealth.

Q. *Can you ever remember a time when you didn't have much money? If there was such a time, in terms of a sense of values, do you think you were happier when you had none or are you happier now that you do?*

A. It sounds kind of trite to say it but I don't think there's any correlation between money and happiness. Some of the happiest people I know don't have anything— and most people I know with money are very miserable. But there have been many times when I didn't have money.

My family was extremely poor. When I was about

twelve years old, I won a scholarship to a fine prep
school and I was about the only poor kid in the school.
Everyone else there had money. They had beautiful
clothes and many had chauffeurs, nice homes, and all
that. I really felt out of place! One of the things that
got me started gambling was I found I could separate
the kids from some of their money through football
pools, betting on election results, that kind of thing.

I never had any money as a kid other than what I
won gambling. Because of my desire for rapid growth,
when I started in business I kept myself pretty well
stripped financially, plowing everything back into the
business. Then I had some financial reverses.

Of course, no one likes being poor, but the wonderful
realization that a Christian has is that if he's in the
will of God, then everything else is really secondary.
Then you're going to have inner peace, tranquility, purpose, and meaning in life. Whether or not you have
money is really not the key issue.

Q. *What about your attitudes toward acquiring things? Now
that you can pretty much have what you want in a material sense, are you tempted to constantly gratify your
desires or those of your family when they ask for cars,
clothes, and a new house?*

A. That's one of the toughest things, I think, because
there's a great amount of prayer, will power, and resistance to temptation involved in this. There's a real
danger of losing one's sense of values. Actually, it's a
combination of several things. I think there's the matter
of stewardship which any thinking, committed Christian
takes seriously—the fact that what we have is not ours.
No matter how much money God makes available to

us, how much can we properly spend of that? Then there's a very practical consideration—the effect on the kids. That has always been uppermost in our minds.

Q. *That was going to be my next question. How do you deal with your children on the subject of money?*

A. Many good Christians I know, who are well to do, have problems with their kids. The problems range anywhere from worldliness to spiritual indifference or rebellion, even hostility. This can happen to good people who are solid Christians! Our observation was that money can be more of a bane than a blessing. So we decided that this matter of money was important. We had to take it seriously and endeavor not to spoil our kids.

Q. *How does that work out practically in your family? Do you give your children an allowance? When they ask to use the car or have a car do you buy them one—or tell them to save their money and get one themselves?*

A. You probably won't believe this when I tell you. Our kids have had a nice home to live in. In that respect they've been pretty well off. But we have given them a very modest allowance which would be on the low side in their particular circle of friends. They go to a Christian school where most of the families are not well off, but most of them get higher allowances than our kids do. We just think it's bad for them to have too much spending money. Our children have led a very sheltered life. They have always been in evangelical churches and schools. And they've never had television because I think television spoils people and it drains an awful lot of time. But our kids are spending much of their time reading and a fair amount of that time reading the Scriptures. So I can honestly say that their interests, with the exception of sports—and the boys' interest in sports in particular—all the other interests of our seven kids are totally Christ-oriented.

Q. *Did you find a rebellion, a resistance to this approach when you started—or did you just start this at the beginning and this has been the only kind of life they've ever known?*

A. When we finally had a vote on whether to have television, they voted against it! And we've tried to teach them realistically about money and what it does for them. And because we love them we didn't want to spoil them.

Q. *But how do you do that, Art? Kids are kids. They see a sports car, they see some clothes, and they know all they would have to do is write a check or ask you to write one.*

A. Well, we wouldn't do it. We wouldn't do it. On the matter of a car, we made a deal with our kids which they accepted, with some enthusiasm I might say. Here's what we do with cars. We really have two deals with cars.

Some years ago we told them they would get so much credit for each book they read on an approved reading list. The credit would apply toward a car. So that if they read well, they could drive well when they got older. If they read like a bum, they'd drive like a bum, if at all. I think it was a $10 credit for each book or something like that. But we didn't do our part. It took a lot of paperwork to keep them going. So we canceled that. Meanwhile, they developed good reading habits so it served its purpose.

But then we came up with a much simpler approach which today I'm sure most Christians would consider very oppressive. The deal we made with our kids was that if until they finished college they wouldn't drink, smoke, dance or go to movies, they'd get a new car when they got out of college. The kind of car they got would depend on subjective considerations such as their spiritual commitment, their attitude, and their grades. So, conceivably, they could get a Mercedes or they might get a Chevrolet. Meanwhile, when they finished their freshman year in college, they could get a used car if they didn't slip along the way. They think that's a great idea.

When I became a Christian back in the 1950s, the standards Christians had then, rightly or wrongly, were a lot different. Hardly any Christians went to movies or danced or drank—and today I would say the majority of Christians feel those prohibitions are legalistic or whatever. While I agree with that I would still say it's better not to involve ourselves in these things. But we've never had a problem with that. We think it's healthy and that's how the kids get their cars.

Q. *And having met your kids, Art, let me say they are the most well-mannered, alert, intelligent, handsome, and spiritually mature children I think I've ever known.*

A. That's been one of the most humbling and rewarding things—remarks like you've made here and what others have told us. It's been very gratifying. So I don't think money has been a problem. The kids have never had a lot of money but they've lived well. If there's a flaw here, I think kids need to learn how to handle money. Now whether they learn better with $20 a week than with $2 a week, I don't know. Maybe they learn better with the larger amount. But maybe they should learn how to handle $2 a week before they have the opportunity to handle the bigger amounts.

Q. *Let's change the subject a moment. Can you remember times when you were angry with God? When your house burned to the ground, was that one of those times?*

A. I can honestly say, Cal, that the Lord has given us a great equanimity so that nothing has been terribly disturbing in terms of calamity, adversity or apparent tragedies. In fact, God's brought me through three economic stages. I was poor for most of my life, then for a period of time things went phenomenally well in the business, the family, health. No problems. Nothing. People would ask me how things were going and I'd say, "Boy, I hope things don't get any better. I don't think that I could stand it!"

Then in a period of about a year we were hit with several things simultaneously. This was late '72. For example, I had gone fifteen years without missing a single day's work because of illness. I never got sick. I thought people who became ill were lazy or weren't motivated or something. I never believed in it. Then, in a year's time I was in the hospital twice. My wife then had very serious brain surgery for a massive tumor and we almost lost her. That was about the same time, in mid-'73. Then we were burned out of our home where we had lived for ten years. It was a very nice home. Then, as a result of a precipitous drop in the price of our stock, I lost about $300 million. It was about a million dollars a day for almost a year. And all that happened at the same time. In the midst of this, Bill Bright (President of Campus Crusade for Christ International) was visiting me and he asked me how I felt and I could honestly tell him I never felt better in my life. I just felt wonderful because I had been prepared by learning a scriptural truth that *things* really aren't important. It's nice to have things. Like anyone else, I enjoy nice things. But I think if we really believe that things aren't all that important, if we only have them to enjoy for awhile, fine, then that's all right, too. I believe with Paul that we can really be content in whatsoever state we are in.

But along the same line, I've learned that the thread which runs through not only my life but through every Christian's life is Romans 8:28, that all things work together for good (to those who love God and are called according to his purpose). If we in fact believe that, then we're not tempted to curse God or lose faith when difficulties come. Then we can really say, "Lord, I don't understand it, but I know it must be for the best, so I accept it and I thank You for it."

Q. *Do you find that easier to do when you're rich or poor?*

A. I don't know. I'm not sure there is any correlation. I do think there are some advantages to both. Money provides more convenience. It provides more options—more responsibility. You have a lot more tough decisions to make. There are more of them. And they are God-given responsibilities for stewardship—how you handle the money and the people to whom you are responsible and how you handle your time. The person who has nothing and works for $100 a week, he does his job well and that's it. He's pretty much on his own. But the more you have, the more responsible you must be.

Q. *About your wife, Nancy. During this period when she was about to have brain surgery and you almost lost her, how did you feel about that in your innermost self? Did you strike any deals with God? Did you promise him anything as some people might have done in your situation?*

A. No, I don't think so. No.

Q. *How did you pray? What did you ask for?*

A. We had about a week's notice before the surgery. Nancy was having noises in her head and some problems with her hearing. She went to several doctors and specialists and when it was diagnosed, she went right into the hospital. So we really didn't have a lot of advance notice.

Q. *So, what did you pray about? I suppose you considered more than once the possibility she might be taken from you.*

A. Oh, yes. The doctors made it clear it was a high risk situation. She was on the operating table for eight and one half hours. Then she was in intensive care for some time. But the Lord was very real and, again, all things work together for good and that helps. I guess, though, there's a fine line between . . . I don't know if "resigned" is the word . . . but really accepting God's will and what some people perceive as fatalism or what some Christians might perceive as callousness. People think you're supposed to shout or get excited when your kid is hit by a car or when your wife has a brain tumor. I'm sure some emotion such as concern or compassion or love is allowed, but I don't really think any situation calls for getting emotionally upset or yelling and that kind of thing.

Q. *Still, you must have had some kind of concern for Nancy.*

A. Oh, sure . . .

Q. *What did you pray about? Did your stomach get upset, especially during her surgery?*

A. I prayed for the Lord's will, that he would guide the surgeon's hands. I'm known for going way back and recalling the worst things that ever happened to me, humanly speaking. I never forget adversity or calamity or whatever. I'd go back with the benefit of hindsight and apply Romans 8:28—and it's amazing that one thing after another worked out. It sometimes took months or frequently years, but the outcome was invariably an improvement. In none of these cases could I see at the time how they would be a blessing in disguise.

Just one illustration. This has nothing to do with Nancy in the hospital. Shortly after I became a Christian, I had a lot of ambitious ideas about making a great deal of money for the Lord. So in the course of pursuing a project I thought would make a lot of money for the Lord's work, I bought a small chain of supermarkets. Right away I found I had to make a decision because beer was being sold in those supermarkets. People told me if I cut the beer I'd go out of business. So I thought, *Well, while I'm not uptight about people taking a drink if they want to, I am against Christians*

selling it. I'd been in that business, too, before I was a Christian. By the way, I even had a night club for awhile, so I developed some convictions about this whole area. But I went in and threw the beer out. Sure enough, those people were right. The next thing I knew I was out of business. It was a costly experience.

However, again with the benefit of hindsight, that was one of the best things that ever happened to me. If I hadn't obeyed and if I'd compromised on that, maybe I'd still be a grocer! And I'm sure I wouldn't have enjoyed it nearly as much as I enjoy what I'm doing.

So the Lord had something better for me. That wasn't

the right thing for me to do anyhow. So it was a good experience.

Q. *We've been talking a lot about your strengths, about God's strength in your life. Everyone has weaknesses. What's one of yours?*

A. I think you should probably ask someone else . . . my greatest strength or greatest weakness. It's difficult to be objective about oneself.

Q. *Maybe Nancy has told you what she thinks it is!*

A. She wishes I wouldn't use toothpicks in public! But I'm sure I have worse habits than that. I may be too goal-oriented, but I don't think that's necessarily bad. I think there's a very thin line between what could be considered a weakness or a strength.

I had a very interesting dinner last night with a man who was in the Nixon Administration with Chuck Colson. This guy thinks very highly of Chuck and he said he always considered him very bright, but hard driving—bordering on ruthless. I guess Chuck would say the same thing about himself.* But goal orientation or drive . . . there's a fine line between that and ruthlessness. So any of our instincts, unless they are Spirit-controlled, can very easily become a weakness. Then there are times when I take the Lord off the throne and place myself there. But I'm sure there are worse things than that. I just don't know how I would objectively assess my greatest strength or greatest weakness. You'll have to find that out from someone else.

---

* See the interview with Chuck Colson which appears later in the book.

Charles Colson

Prison Fellowship

Charles Colson and friends

It's been more than five years since news of one of the greatest conversion stories in history hit the front pages of America's newspapers. Charles W. Colson, to whom so many evil deeds had been ascribed that Satan himself would be envious (and more were ascribed by reporters, it should be mentioned, than by prosecutors), Charles Colson, the White House hatchet man, Charles Colson who is supposed to have said (but never did) that he would run over his own grandmother to get Richard Nixon elected President— Charles Colson had been born again!

The details of that conversion are spelled out in the best selling book, *Born Again,* and in the movie by the same name.

But what has happened to Colson since *Born Again?*

Colson devotes most of his time and much of his money to Prison Fellowship, a unique program that has won the endorsement of Norman Carlson, the director of the Federal Bureau of Prisons. Where government programs have failed to rehabilitate men and women who have entered America's jails and prisons, Colson's Prison Fellowship offers the only hope for reducing prison populations, changing men's hearts, and keeping the revolving door of many prisons from going around and around.

Under the Prison Fellowship program, specially selected

men and women are brought from the Federal prisons to Washington for a two-week period of Bible study, discipleship, fellowship, and Christian love. Then at the end of that time, they are sent back to their prisons as leaders for Jesus Christ to win and disciple other men and women in his name.

While Colson is not alone among people who minister to those in prison, because of his name and influence he is having an impact on a nationwide scale that is unequaled in the history of the prisons of this country.

Q. *You've said that the past year of your life has been your most difficult. What do you mean by that?*

A. Well, yes, difficult in the sense that we've had many more challenges and tremendous opportunities for service. And yet, great frustration because we can't meet all the challenges.

It's been extremely difficult in terms of the long hours. I've never worked so hard in my life. I don't have a weekend anymore—I've forgotten what a weekend is like! If I'm home, not traveling or speaking, I'll be working at my desk . . . writing, reading papers from the office, trying to read a book a week (which I've sort of set as a goal but I don't always make it). And it's difficult in the sense of not being able to do all the things I really believe God is providing opportunities for me to do.

We are building a ministry from scratch and we're experiencing all the growing pains. We've had a major motion picture to contend with, and I've had to work on the script. Sometimes when you try to do too many things, you don't do anything well. That's a frustration.

Q. *Some people say that when Satan has a hold of you, before you come to know Christ, that you don't realize it but later you are much more aware of his attacks against you. Do you feel a real burden, a weight on your shoulders, a responsibility to people looking to you as an example?*

A. Certainly. That's the most awesome aspect of what I'm doing. This summer will be my sixth anniversary as a Christian (1979). It's still pretty new. I've had to take kind of a cram course, both in help from the brothers and then studying and in straightening out all the disciplines and habits in my life.

I realize that a great number of believers are watching to see if Chuck Colson's for real. A lot of people weren't believers but now are because they've read *Born Again.* Literally thousands, probably, are watching to see what happens to the guy who introduced them to Christ. And even more significant than any of that is the fact that a big hunk of the secular world, the nonbelievers, the disbelievers who don't want to believe, are just waiting for me to fall and then they will be able to say, "We were right all along."

If I don't fall, a lot of those people are liable to be dragged kicking and screaming into the kingdom. And so there's a huge weight on my shoulders, and it affects my life in a lot of ways, besides those obvious to the eye.

I mean, I don't go out to cocktail parties, but that doesn't bother me because I never did before. I didn't like them, preconversion, so that's not paying much of a price. But I'll be nervous driving an automobile, because I think to myself, *If I am driving along and a child jumps out in the middle of the road and I hit that child, people are going to say, aha, he wasn't really a Christian.* And so I begin to get a little spooked in a lot of ways I ought not to. I ought to be a little freer as I live my life.

And I've never liked publicity—the public glare. I find myself right in the middle of it! I was hit with a pie last week. My old instinctive reaction would have been to take the guy apart. Instead, I felt a great peace about it, not angry.

Q. *You mentioned some things that you had to give up, some disciplines you had to accomplish. Could you elaborate on those?*

A. Sure. One is smoking. But I finally think, with the Lord's help, I have that under control. That's always been a problem for me.

Q. *Was there more than health reasons involved in that? Perhaps the image smoking projected?*

A. Well, it's a witness. If eating meat will cause my brother to stumble, I won't eat meat. And so it's the stumbling block issue. I don't read anything in the Bible that says you can't smoke. I do read things in the Bible that say you can't overindulge and be slothful and eat too much. And most of the people who've come up to me with nasty remarks about my smoking have had huge stomachs protruding out over their belts. But, so be it.

I mean, I was comforted watching the story of Martin Luther King on television to discover that he was a closet smoker, but couldn't be seen publicly. However, the Lord is whipping that for me and I'm getting rid of the addiction, which it is. For health reasons and to the extent that I might smoke publicly, it would be a witness problem.

Now, I'm thinking more of the discipline of the guy who hits you in the face with a pie. I was a captain in the Marines. In the old days I would have turned around and clobbered someone who did that to me. And I thought I would have to restrain myself if it ever happened—but I found out I didn't have to restrain myself at all. There was perfect peace about it. Happily, I had just been reading Bonhoeffer's *The Cost of Discipleship* where he says violence begets violence and violence is defeated by a nonviolent reaction. And so I told this kid that Jesus forgave him and I left him—I hope with a nagging thought in his mind that there's something real to this Christianity.

Q. *And maybe you left him with egg on his face!*

A. I told him, "All I have to do is go upstairs to my hotel room and take a shower and I'll be clean. You have to do a lot more than that to get yourself clean."

Q. *As you look back on the White House years, what differences are there between then and now in the temptations you face?*

A. This is a much more painful life, because then I could and did cut any corners I needed to if there was a worthy end. When I was in the White House it never bothered me in the slightest.

Now I find I can't really cheat even if I think I can get away with it totally in man's eyes—because I know the Lord is watching. And that puts me on a pretty tight leash because when I want to do something I have to stop and ask, "Is it right?" I never did that in the White House. Now even if I thought I could fool the entire world, I still would have trouble doing it because I would know that something was between me and the Lord. He knows, so I can't get away with it.

Q. *A lot of people look at the "born again" experience as the beginning of a life of perfection. Has it been easier or more difficult since you accepted Christ?*

A. Well, it's been both, Cal. It's a lot easier in the sense that if one can learn to trust in the Lord and to accept his sovereignty and his ways, many things that one otherwise would have struggled with, he no longer struggles with. Psalm 37 gives a pretty good prescription for trusting in the Lord, resting in the Lord, and not fretting yourself—which, as David says, leads into evil doing. So, in a sense, there's a lot of peace when I simply trust God in everything.

By the other standards, however, I struggle a lot more because I am trying to be pleasing to God which I cannot be. I know I've sinned. One Christian scholar said, "I sin at least 100 times a day." And Luther talked about this when he said, "Sin boldly. . . ." That's not a license to cheap grace, but the apostle Paul said, "I die daily." So it is a struggle, because I'm struggling more to be God's man. On the other hand there's a certain peace about it because I don't feel that it's all resting on my shoulders. You and I can feel we are God's instruments and he's sovereign and so we can trust him for the really big plays.

Q. *What depresses you? And how do you handle it?*

A. What depresses me? Well, some of the same things that have always depressed me: not being able to get all my work done, not having enough hours in the day, not feeling that I've done a good enough job at something (I'm a perfectionist). The public spotlight depresses me.

A year or so ago a woman came up to me and started pulling on my sleeve—and she yanked a button off my coat, all in love. She loved me so much she wanted me to come to her church to speak. And for an instant I was tempted to throw her down on the ground and step on her! That would have confirmed that Chuck Colson runs over grandmothers! But I'm only human and so much of that can sometimes really get under my skin. People gawk and stare at me constantly and I feel like a monkey in a zoo! There are days when that has depressed me enormously.

Then there are days when I don't feel I'm living the life that I ought to be living as a Christian. One thing Doug Coe* does which is very helpful and I try doing it, is start every day by saying, "Is Christ enough for me for everything?" And if I answer that question honestly, I will have to answer "No." During the day, I have to have a little loving pat from my wife or have someone say a nice word to me. During the day someone has to say, "Man, that was a good speech you gave last week, Chuck."

But is Christ sufficient for *everything* in my life? And if I really examine myself or hold myself accountable

---

* Head of Fellowship Foundation in Washington and a member of Colson's small prayer group that also includes former Senator Harold Hughes, former Congressman Graham Purcell, and former Representative, now Governor, Al Quie of Minnesota.

in a small group the way John Wesley did, then I don't feel so good and that can be depressing.

The biggest single depression I have is the inability to do as much as I want to do—and that sometimes gets me very depressed. And the public spotlight. Many times I can get used to it—there's no problem and I can handle it. But the twenty-four-hour-a-day variety is heavy.

Q. *How about inadequacy? Do you feel inadequate? Do you have a problem with self-worth? Many people wouldn't think so since you're such a household name.*

A. Yeah, sure, but that gives you all the more problems because you say, "Why me, Lord?" And why should I be so good to be held up on a pedestal for other people to admire and emulate?

My favorite poem is one of Dietrich Bonhoeffer's. I can't recite it to you verbatim but I can give you the gist of it. It's entitled "Who am I?" or a better way to put it, "Who *Am* I?" You'll find it in the preface to *The Cost of Discipleship.* Just to paraphrase, he says, "Am I the man they say I am, who stands fearlessly beside my comrades in need, who flinches not in the face of battle, . . . " and he goes on describing what people think of him. And then he says, "Or, am I the one who recoils in terror, who lies asleep restless at night, who longs to be a million miles from here (he's writing it from prison), who is a wretched person" and he describes himself. And the final thing, "Who am I? The man they say I am or the man I know I am? Whatever the answer, God, all I know is that I am Thine."

It's a tremendous poem. But it is the conflict that

goes on inside a person who is held up as a leader from whom others draw inspiration and strength. The more other people draw it from you, sometimes I think the less you have inside of you to give to yourself. Maybe that's why the Lord had to get away and sometimes didn't want people touching him. And so, of course, that's a constant battle. I don't have any problem with self-worth in the normal, conventional sense, but I do in the celebrity sense.

Q. *What about those moments when you lose your temper? What kind of person are you during those times? Do you lose your temper every now and then?*

A. Not very often. I never have. But when I do it's usually spectacular.

Q. *How? Francis Schaeffer talks about having this potted plant he now keeps safely on his desk because whenever he got mad he used to fling it across the room. His wife, Edith, would come and pick it up and replace it in the pot. Now he says every time he looks at it he is reminded of his limitations, of his sinfulness. Do you have a potted plant in your life?*

A. Not as such, no. I don't think I've ever broken anything. I probably have kicked an occasional piece of furniture, though. I'd kick a dog if I had him around! Oh, I'll just rant and rave and pound my fist on the desk, get blue in the face, and go take a long walk. But I don't often lose my temper. I never have. You see, I don't really fit this book, because as I walked to work this morning across the river . . . !

"I have the only pardon . . ."

Q. *You can do that over some parts of the polluted Potomac! Do you have a secret desire in your heart to be pardoned for your Watergate offenses?*

A. By the State?

Q. *Yes.*

A. No. I have the only pardon that a guy could ask for. No, as a matter of fact I was invited by a top official of the State of Virginia to write a letter to the Governor in December, 1977, just before Mills Godwin went out of office. I was told that if I asked for the restoration of my civil liberties in Virginia, they'd be granted. And I refused to write the letter because the laws of the State are archaic. The only reason I could get my civil liberties back is that I'm Chuck Colson, celebrity. But what about the poor guy (who leaves prison) who goes back to work in a coal mine in Southwest Virginia, who doesn't have a friend in the State House? The rest of his life he can't vote. And so I refused to write the Governor. I want my civil liberties back. I want to be able to vote in Virginia. But I want it when they change the stinking law, not when they make an exception for a famous person. The same would apply with a Federal pardon.

I think every ex-convict who has been out of prison for a period of five years ought to be automatically eligible for a pardon so that society can wipe the slate clean. Why hold that over a person's head into his grave? Many men have come out of prison and made good lives for themselves. Some have come out and gone back. One reason they go back is that there's no hope on the outside. There's no hope for that pardon.

Q. *Have you made much progress in reconciling yourself with former enemies, besides Arthur Burns, the Federal Reserve Chairman? Someone, perhaps, like Watergate Special Prosecutor Leon Jaworski? (Colson shifts in his chair at the mention of Jaworski's name. The two have differed sharply over the substance of a meeting in Jaworski's office. Colson has said Jaworski offered to allow him to plead guilty to a misdemeanor and other charges would be dropped. Jaworski staunchly maintains he did no such thing and held out for a felony plea. Colson has said he chose to plead guilty to a felony. Jaworski contends he so pled because he was given no other choice.) Yes, Jaworski bristles when I mention your name to him!*

A. I'm not bristling. That's his problem. Well, it takes two to make a reconciliation. I mean, I hold no animosity toward Mr. Jaworski in my heart. Though if there were any man on this earth toward whom I would have a right to feel animosity, it would be Leon Jaworski. I don't hold any. Obviously he holds a lot. And I've forgiven him. I'm clean as far as the Lord's concerned. And someday for his sake, I hope Mr. Jaworski will feel the same way.

Q. *Have you made any approaches to him? Have you ever written him a letter? Phone call?*

A. I tried to. Harold Hughes was in touch with him once about getting us together, but Mr. Jaworski was too busy.

Q. *I suggested that once to him and he said, "Well, maybe someday."*

A. When I prove myself. There are some people I've had great healing with, both small and large (names). But it will come someday with Mr. Jaworski.

Q. *Many people have been critical of the evangelical star system. A well-known person finds Christ and he is thrown on stage and in front of TV cameras to give a testimony he often has not developed. Is there room for such a star system and are you one of those stars?*

A. The National Religious Broadcasters Convention of 1978 was sort of the ultimate, the big show, the biggest show in town. We've sold the chickens, come in off the farm, and now we're in the city. We're parading all the superstars before the public daily. It's great until you're in a position to know all those individuals as intimately as I know them—and realize they all have feet of clay just like I do. And why do we hold them up and exalt them?

I read a news story recently about a little man named Louis Esposito, who for 36 years held down three jobs to pay for medical care for his daughter who was in a coma. And the point I made in a recent speech about this was that when Louis Esposito dies, as he did two weeks ago, I suspect that as he walked across that line the Lord was there to say, "Well done, good and faithful servant." Now they'll never make any books about Esposito, or movies, but that's the Christlike life: service. Being a servant. I think it's unfortunate that we are so conformed to the world that we equate fame with righteousness or we believe that we have to keep showing the world that God really succeeds. It's really a weakness in our own faith.

The Word of God should be sufficient for all things.

A relationship with the person of Christ is all that man should need. And yet we seem to feel that to evangelize the world we need to constantly hold up the latest exhibit and say, "You see, God is still real because, look. He took this filthy sinner and turned him into a saint." So we constantly look for the athlete, movie star, ex-convict, Hell's Angel, Manson killer and the worse the guy before, the better.

I listened to Senator Mark Hatfield tell how bad I was when he introduced me last week—and how much he now loves me, to show the dramatic change. Afterwards I said, "Mark, did you really think all those things about me when we were both in politics?" He said, "Well, maybe not." There's a tendency to overdramatize the bad in the past, the good of the present, to show the contrast which is really a reflection on our own faith, the adequacy of our own faith.

On the other hand, I understand the system and it can have some merit. I can tell in my own case that I'm a layman and having come from where I've come, many people can identify with me. I'm sure there are many people who came to Christ reading *Born Again,* reading about me or hearing me speak . . . I know this because they've told me. . . . Those were people who were never touched by any minister or religious professional—because they felt that was his job. But they could find an identification with me. Now in that sense the celebrity business is healthy, because it is winning people who might not otherwise have been won to Christ. And there is a peer identification that is possible, but we should not exalt the people in the process. To me that's the danger.

Q. *What do you and your wife, Patty, fight about?*

"He saw a trophy"

A. What do we fight about?

Q. *How do you fight with your wife?*

A. Oh, we sometimes get mad at each other and pout. We don't fight physically. Like any other wife, she gets a little put out when I don't pay enough attention to her. We don't fight over money. We don't fight over many of the things people normally fight over because we do most everything together. When we do get angry with each other, it's usually because an innocent remark in misinterpreted. Our fights are kind of like summer storm clouds. They pass quickly. No real battles.

Q. *One of the most frequently asked questions about you concerns your wife. People want to know where she is spiritually. How is she doing? Is she getting the input, the growth as a Christian?*

A. Yes. She's at Bible study this morning and has turned into quite a Bible student. We pray together a great deal at home. She resents the "evangelical clubbishness" which I do as well. When someone comes up to her and says, "When did you find the Lord?" she'll often reply, "I haven't"—just to watch that person go into orbit. As a matter of fact we were with a couple recently and the man asked her, "When did you find the Lord?" As he did he got this gleeful look in his eyes and he rubbed his hands together.

Patty replied, "I haven't," and he started to witness to her! He said, "Well, there's no time like the present. We may not be here in a few more hours. Maybe the Lord's coming back and all you gotta do is bow your head and pray." Of course she was laughing inside, hysterically. She could hardly contain herself. Knowing her as I do I suspect she has always been a far better Christian than the man who was trying to "club" her.

But suddenly he had stars in his eyes. He saw a trophy. "I'm going to be the one who leads Patty Colson to Christ." She was just putting him on. And I thought he got what he deserved, because when you walk up to someone and ask, "When did you find the Lord?" it's like saying, "Tell me your story and I'll test you to see if it's as good as mine."

To me, that is the poorest type of evangelism. Our lives should be a living witness, a model. And we're not a living witness when we go up with our own code words to see if people know the password to get into the fraternity. So Patty resents that approach, although she treats it good naturedly.

Q. *What about the future? Is it Prison Fellowship forever?*

A. One day at a time is what the Scriptures say. I certainly have myself very deeply committed to what I'm doing here because I've put everything I have into it: my own money, all of my time, my energies. I've turned down lots of things in the private sector that might be very attractive. So I will continue to do this as long as I believe it's God's will for my life.

The desperate condition the world is in today grows out of the fact that we are all victims of what Jacques Ellul calls the "political illusion." We think there's a political solution to all problems. To go back to the Psalms, 118 and 146, we are told to take refuge in the Lord. Do not trust in princes and kings. I believe that this is a message I am called to deliver. I don't know whether you would call it prophetic. But it is to shatter people's beliefs that there are government answers to all problems. And to demonstrate that the gospel of Jesus Christ is not only the salvation of man but the hope of mankind. I want to get people weaned away from this knee-jerk reaction we have in the United States that when there's a problem, such as not enough rain in Northern California, government has to do something.

It's very much like Elijah going to the people of Israel after a three-year drought and saying, "Put your trust in the Lord your God or the prophets of Baal." Choose. In other words, turn away from false idols. The people turned away and the rains came. But we have an idea government can solve all our problems. I don't believe it can. I don't believe it can even begin to do so. So the work I believe God has called me to is to try to show the world that the gospel of Jesus Christ lived out in our lives and carried out into the world can make the difference where man's ways fail. As long as there's a mission to try to show that, as long as there is need in the prisons, I can't imagine wanting to do anything else.

Valery Moorhead

and

Ellen Armstrong

Two Congressional Wives

Carlos and Val Moorhead

Jill Briscoe, Mrs. Jack Kemp and Val Moorhead at a Bible study
for congressional wives at Fellowship House in Washington, D.C.
Ray Thomas photos

There was a time when "divorced" ranked just behind "crook" as a label unconditionally guaranteed to be politically fatal. And while constituents viewed extramarital affairs as something *they* might occasionally excuse, politicians in Washington were expected to live by much higher standards. Well, as the commercial says, "We've come a long way, baby."

The recent well-publicized nocturnal activities of the now-sober ex-Congressman Wilbur Mills with Fannie Fox and Wayne Hayes with Elizabeth Ray are rare only in the sense that their sin was blatant. Other quiet affairs continue in Washington, unnoticed or unreported.

The pressures on Washington marriages have never been greater. Even marriages made in heaven back home can be unmade after a single term in the Nation's Capital.

But, as usual, the scandals and the headlines don't tell the whole story. Just as there are many decent politicians so, too, there are some good marriages that have grown and prospered in Washington's tough soil.

I talked with two women, Mrs. Carlos Moorhead (Valery), whose husband represents a Southern California district which includes Glendale, and Mrs. Bill Armstrong (Ellen), whose husband represented at the time of our interview a district that includes the Denver, Colorado, suburb of Aurora. He was elected to the U.S. Senate in the November, 1978, elections. Both are Republicans. Both women were divorced prior to becoming Christians, but the stories of what they learned from those marriages and how they have built their current marriages on a much stronger foundation should encourage people who have given up on anything decent happening in Washington.

Valery Moorhead's husband, Carlos, is a three-term Republican Congressman from Southern California. Prior to that, he spent six years in the State legislature and before that he was an attorney in Glendale for over twenty years.

Valery taught school for ten years in the Torrance, California, Unified School District, sixth grade level. She is a graduate of the University of Southern California with a degree in Education.

Most of her work now revolves around Christian activities such as Community Bible Study, Congressional Wives Fellowship Group, and a study of Dr. Francis Schaeffer's books which meets in the home of Mrs. Jack Kemp, wife of the Buffalo, New York, Congressman.

Q. *What are some of the pressures that face a political wife in Washington? They must be different than the pressures of the California legislature, aren't they?*

A. When you say different than California, do you mean being a political wife in California versus being a political wife here?

Q. *That and the unique pressures of Washington, not only on your marriage, but on you as individuals and on your growth together.*

A. I've spoken to many women over the past several years, and the thing I notice in a general way is that women struggle with nonidentity, not really knowing exactly what they are supposed to do or not being satisfied with their roles as Congressional wives. Congressional husbands are so busy, number one. They're involved with constituents or involved on the Hill. A congressman is in the limelight most of the time. So a lot of women who are not Christians, and some who are, find that the role of the pretty little wife who just comes along for the show is not enough for them. And so they become frustrated with who they are and what they're supposed to do—trying to find their own identity and self-worth. I think this really impresses me about the women I talk to.

However, women who know Christ, know who they are. They seem to be better able to handle the fact that their husbands are gone or busy and all these other things. Sure, they feel the pain of it and the loneliness. They feel the anxiety and all the things that everyone else feels, but because they have Christ in their lives they have Someone to go to and they can deal with this—and they also know who they are! Christ gives us our own identity. I see a difference. I really do see a difference between how women who know Christ handle the problems—and those who don't have the Lord in their lives. I know that it's an enormous difference.

Q. *Having said that and knowing these things, in your humanity, does it ever get to you sometimes? Do you ever wish you could go back to California and have a nice, simple life, see each other every day?*

A. Certainly I do. I feel those pressures. Going places with one's husband and then not really being able to finish a meal together can be frustrating. Someone will invariably come up and interrupt us—and want to talk to him about business. You do have those moments when you think, *Wouldn't it be nice if life were simple again?* But there are compensations, so many wonderful things about this life. When you weigh them, the pluses far outweigh the minuses for me.

Q. *Are the compensations found only in service, only in Carlos's being who he is, having the influence that he does?*

A. I think I find most of the compensations in service. Being in Washington . . . it's just an extremely exciting place to live. Here one can meet people, other congressmen and their wives from all over, every state of the nation, international people. Such an opportunity just doesn't come to one very often. The fact that we can be invited to the White House or the State Department and meet interesting people from the Pentagon . . . almost every Washington party we might go to has fascinating people. And you'd be amazed at the opportunities to witness at some of these parties—perhaps not openly and directly, but indirectly. Sometimes there are opportunities to witness directly.

And then there are the cultural aspects. There are untold opportunities to become involved in this way. There are so many ways I can fulfill myself and compensations for the bad things. I'm in the middle of this hub of the world and for anyone not to seize this opportunity would be quite unusual. As I said before, I see many women who don't know God, who don't see God. They just see the bad things.

Q. *Do you ever think that maybe Washington is the most unreal city in the country? Much of the rest of the country* *doesn't share your enthusiasm for this city or the people in it, particularly those in government.*

A. Of course, my husband and I sometimes feel the same way. My husband is fortunate because he seems to enjoy quite a bit of popularity in his district. People really like him. They know he's honest and they know he's doing a good job. But I've found that most people like to believe in their own congressman, that he is honest and doing a good job—but that all the other congressmen are not! It's literally true. So the general image of politicians, especially in the wake of Watergate, is not good.

Most of the people I've met here in Washington are really of high calibre. There are many Christian people here whom the public doesn't know about. And I think it's exciting because they (the Christians) seem to be coming out more and more with their belief in Christ—congressmen and senators and others. There seems to be a greater openness in this whole area. It's too bad that people generalize so much and think all the people in Washington, all politicians, are not honorable. Or they attribute some ulterior motive for doing what politicians do. There seems to be a negative connotation surrounding all politicians. This is wrong. Our country really needs to undergird all elected officials. We really need to try to put the trust back there again. True, the politicians have to earn it—they have to deserve it. But so much of the criticism is undeserved and general in nature. . . .

Q. *What do you and Carlos argue about?*

A. I suppose we argue about things most married couples argue about—our use of time, sometimes. He, of course, feels the demand and the need to go out into his district. I try to be as open and as giving about his devotion to duty as I can be—but sometimes we run into conflicts and it can be a problem. I've learned more and more as I've gone along . . . I have a story to tell you about that if you want to hear it sometime.

Q. *I'll hear it right now if you'll tell me.*

A. When I first came here I really had a struggle. I was a brand new Christian—I'd only been a Christian for a couple of years.

Q. *How long ago was that?*

A. I became a Christian in the spring of 1970, so when we came here I'd been a Christian only a couple of years. Being in a strange place and not really having any friends, being left alone—especially in the beginning—was rough. The first term any congressman is in office, he really has to do a great deal of work. He has to lay the groundwork because people don't know him that well. Carlos had to be gone a lot and I had a terrible struggle with loneliness and not liking to be left alone. When you ask me what we argued about, that really was it more than anything. And it wasn't so much that the argument was bad—it was what was going on inside of me when he came back.

I was storing up all this resentment because things would happen while he was gone. The basement would flood, Paul would break his wrist, the dog would run away . . . all these things seemed to happen when he was gone. So here I was, feeling very competent because I could handle these things myself, but inside I was really resenting that I didn't have a husband around to take care of these things when I needed him.

I guess I really didn't know at that time what to do with my feeling. I even felt guilty because I felt that way. Then he'd come home and it would take me about three days to get it out of my system. At those times I really wasn't very nice to him. I'd pick at him, you know, pick little arguments and somehow all this resentment was coming out. Yet I wasn't able to face him with it and say, "I don't like this." There didn't seem to be any solution to it anyway. So this was a struggle and I know I was making it difficult for Carlos. He couldn't help but think about it the next time he had to leave town. He'd think, *Well, I guess I've got to go through this de-programming for about two or three days after I come back.*

After I struggled with this for quite awhile, through Community Bible Study I learned that you can actually take anything to the Lord and ask him to help you with it. So I definitely claimed Philippians 4:13, "I can do all things through Christ which strengtheneth me." I knew I wasn't doing too well on my own. One night he was due in at midnight and about half an hour before he was ready to come in the driveway, I had been thinking about it a lot. I thought, *I'm just going to trust the Lord and give this to him and see what happens.* Obviously I couldn't handle the problem myself, so I got down on my knees and prayed for half an hour before he came home. Carlos came in the door and he waited for the crash—and the crash never came!

Two or three days went by and he finally came to me and asked, "Honey, what happened to you? You really seem to have handled it." And I was just so excited because it wasn't something phony that I had to drum up, something I was imagining. It was like a burden had been lifted from me.

Q. *You didn't have to play "The Total Woman" and show up at the door in saran wrap?*

A. No, I didn't! But I felt that I didn't have this resentment and anger. But I realized the real test would come the next time. I do struggle with it still a little, but it is on such a different level now. I can honestly say I am free of the resentment and anger. I still miss Carlos and I still like it better when he's home, but the anger and resentment are gone. That's just one example of how you can really put these things on the Lord and you don't have to handle it any more.

Q. *Do you find it easier now to go to your husband and for him to come to you when you are convicted that one of you has done something wrong, to say you're sorry?*

A. That's one of my problems. Carlos is really wonderful about it. He's always the one who comes and says he's sorry first. I know inside I should do that, too. And I have done it occasionally. But it is hard for me. I struggle with it. Another thing about being a Christian: you don't realize in the beginning that when you accept the Lord, you don't become an instantly perfect person who never makes a mistake. But the Lord has dealt with me in so many ways and brought me through so many things that I really praise him. But as you were saying, I'm still human and I still have weaknesses and areas that need work. And I simply try to give these things over to him one at a time.

Valery Moorhead

Q. *Why do you think you have trouble going to your husband and saying you're sorry?*

A. I suppose it's pride. It probably goes back to my child-hood. My family was quite positive and strong—and right all the time—so I grew up in an atmosphere where people were really very positive about what they thought and felt. I carried that over to my marriage. It's a character flaw I really have to deal with—and ask the Lord to help me do it. So far I haven't made much progress, but I'm praying about it.

Q. *Do you find that you have to defer to your husband in public and only talk about hair styles or clothes or the weather and never get into anything substantive? This has been a criticism of some congressional wives. Do you feel you could give your own opinion publicly on an important subject, particularly if you disagreed with your husband's position?*

A. I've never really had to face that too much since we agree politically about 75 percent of the time, which is a pretty good average. With the 25 percent on which we don't agree I preface my remarks by saying, "This is my own opinion, not my husband's." We do agree most of the time. But I don't ever like to presume that I have a right to speak out on a political issue. Why? Because I really feel strongly that the people have elected my husband. I'm thrilled and happy to help him in any way I can, but as far as my political opinions are concerned, they might be interesting only as a foot-note. I don't feel I should try to persuade people or use my opinion as an influence. A woman's libber would hate that statement! I do think a wife should keep in-

71

formed and be intelligent in her conversations. But as far as using her opinions to influence voters—I think that's wrong. There is a group of wives on the Hill who have banded together to try to do just that, though.

Q. *But you're not inhibited by this. It doesn't take away from your personhood?*

A. No, it doesn't bother me one bit. If someone asks me what I think, I hope I'm honest enough to tell them. But I don't get myself into hot water, because, as I say, most of the time I agree with my husband.

Q. *You were married before and divorced, is that right?*

A. Yes.

Q. *What can you tell me about that? Was it before you became a Christian?*

A. Yes, it was.

Q. *What did you learn in that marriage which you are determined to avoid in this one?*

A. Well, both Carlos and I have been divorced. I had been married for eleven years and had three children. Fortunately by the time of my divorce I had my degree and was teaching so I was able to support myself and still be with my children, basically, when they were home. When I married Carlos, of course I wanted stability for the children. At that point I had taught for a total of ten years. My youngest was 7 and the others were 14 and 16. I was really ready to be a wife, mother, and homemaker again. And so it was a freedom for me not to have to work and to be able to concentrate my energies on being a good wife. Of course, I was also very aware that we both had come out of divorce situations.

It was my good fortune that the wife of my husband's best friend kept after me all the time about Bible studies. At that time I began to attend Bible Study Fellowship in Glendale. This woman was a Christian and a wonderful friend to me. I thought she was fantastic, intelligent, pretty, fun, and weird because she always wanted to go to Bible study! I couldn't quite figure this out. Still, in her loving, caring way, after about seven invitations, she was successful in getting me to go. When I began to go I found that those women really had something I didn't have. Through that group I learned what it was to be a Christian. In time I invited Christ into my life. This happened about two years after we were married.

Q. *Was Carlos a Christian at this time?*

A. Yes, he was. He accepted the Lord when he was in his teens. Now we were both really dedicated to making sure that this marriage worked. Once I understood as a Christian what marriage was really about, I was more determined than ever to make sure that the marriage was going to be on a good foundation. Perhaps the biggest thing I learned was to accept another person exactly as he was and not to try to change him and squeeze him into my mold. I'm not always successful in doing that, but I know enough to try! I know that I can never really change anyone, that Christ must do it. Even though I'm tempted to try, I fail. I made many mistakes in my first marriage. That was one of them. I could not accept my first husband as he was and I wanted to change certain things about him. As a Christian, in this marriage, I'm working on that tendency. I'm trying just to accept my husband for what he is . . . all the wonderful things as well as the things that aren't so wonderful. I realize now that you can't change another person.

Q. *And you're hoping he'll do the same thing for you?*

A. Right. I'm just beginning to learn from the Bible what it means to be a good wife. No one had ever told me, "Submit to your husband." I never understood that before. I always thought that submit meant the doormat syndrome, but it's not that at all! You can be a total, full woman in every sense of the word and yet fulfill God's plan for the family relationship. God must be at the head in Christ—and then the man, the woman, and the children. Once you get that hierarchy straight, things really fall into place. The result is a smoother marriage and a smoother relationship between husband and wife, parents and children—between each one of you and the Lord. It's just that simple.

Q. *What does submit mean to you?*

A. To me, submit means to recognize the headship of the family. When there's a total difference of opinion, when both of us "know we're right," then I must be able to say, "O.K., I'm going to have to give you this problem, husband. This is yours to solve." If he is doing what Christ is telling him to do, he'll take that opinion into consideration in his final decision about the problem.

That's the ideal thing, however. It doesn't always happen that way with us.

Q. *Why do you think so many people in Washington divorce or separate? Even in the Carter Administration with a president who has stressed the family, the Christian values and virtues, there seems to be a great deal of separation and divorce.*

A. In my opinion, I've seen more marriages fall apart because women don't know their position. They don't know who they are. They have this tremendous identity crisis. The husband is extremely busy, very important. He's running around everywhere, going to all these wonderful places. The wife can't handle all that. She may or may not be involved in traveling in these circles. Some wives feel that they live in the shadow of all the important positions their husbands have filled—and they can't handle it. They argue and fight about time, what the husband is doing, and their relationship. Perhaps the man doesn't have enough time for his wife—or he doesn't make time for her.

Another thing I've seen happen is that a wife will refuse to move to Washington. She will prefer living in the home district with her children. She'll say she cannot possibly move the children. Such a woman is putting her children first and her husband second. And that's fatal. I've seen many marriages fall apart for that reason. The man comes to Washington without his wife. He begins working with secretaries who are right up to the minute about what is going on, interested in their work. These obvious opportunities are around him and many men fall prey to that. The wife back home refuses to join him. Such an arrangement spells disaster.

Q. *What about the women in your husband's office? Did you take a little survey? Did you help hire them?*

A. My husband and I have a very loving, trusting relationship. When we came here our former congressman recommended two or three women who had worked for him a long time. They really knew their way around the Hill. So my husband took the man's advice and hired the women. I'm happy to say that most of our office is made up of Christian women and we have a wonderful rapport with one another. They couldn't be finer or more loving to me. It's beautiful. I know that isn't the case in many offices. I also have friends who have real difficulty because there's jealousy between the wife and the staff. And that *is* a problem. Fortunately I'm not bothered by that particular situation.

Q. *What about the future for you? Can you see yourself continuing to revel in the excitement that is Washington for the rest of your life?*

A. I don't know that we'll be here forever. It isn't in our plans. I think my husband is interested in being here as long as his health is good and as long as the people want him. I don't think he plans to be a 75-year-old congressman, not that such men can't be vital. Some of them are wonderful. But Carlos wants us to be able to have some time to ourselves, too. We need time to relax. I rather imagine that when we finish here we'll move back to California.

Q. *Obviously a defeat would force you to move back right away. But do you have a goal . . . another two terms, another three terms, or are you letting the Lord lead in this?*

A. We would certainly like to be here long enough to get our son through college! He's now in high school. That would certainly be one of our goals. But we've talked about it and about how we would feel if we're not re-elected. I'm sure no one likes to be defeated—and especially my husband! He wouldn't like it one bit. But one thing I've learned, whether it's in a relationship with another person or living in a certain place or the type of job I have. This is that the Lord is my only true source of happiness and joy. I really fall on my face when I depend on any one individual for my total happiness. For example, in my first marriage I was happy when my husband was doing the things I wanted—but when he wasn't I was miserable. A Christian knows that no one single individual or circumstance can supply him with everything he needs. Christ is the only One who can do that. So when I look at marriages here in Washington (or all over the country for that matter) I see them falling apart because an individual isn't performing and isn't up to the standard he demands to make himself happy.

Q. *You said you could be happy living just about anywhere. Could Carlos?*

A. I think so. At least I know he'd be happy living anywhere in California! And I'll be happy as long as I'm with him.

Bill and Ellen Armstrong. *Ray Thomas photo*

Ellen Armstrong was born in Wheatland, Wyoming. Her mother and father were homesteaders, but her father walked out on the family when Ellen was three years old. It was up to her mother to fulfill the homestead requirements by living there for the required length of time to make the property their own.

Then they moved to Nebraska where Ellen was raised. Her mother remarried and Ellen says her stepfather is the only real father she's ever known. She only sees her natural father on rare occasions. She claims there is nothing between them, but she says she's not bitter toward him.

Ellen was sixteen years old and a junior in high school when she married a young man who worked in her stepfather's office. She says the marriage was wrong right from the beginning. The end came eight years later. There were no children.

After the divorce, Ellen began flying as a stewardess for Western Airlines. She flew with Western for three years and it was during this time that she met Bill Armstrong. Nearly four years later they were married.

They have two children, sixteen and twelve. The early years were hectic with Ellen returning to school at Denver University, Bill running for and winning a seat in the State legislature, and the birth of their first child. She managed to graduate with her class four years later. Her graduation present to herself and her husband was their second child! Ellen is now the wife of a senator, since Bill defeated Floyd Haskell in the elections of November, 1978. This interview was conducted after Bill had announced his candidacy for the Senate but prior to the election.

Q. *What are some of the unique pressures you face as a congressional wife?*

A. For lack of a better word, Bill is a workaholic. When we lived in Colorado, he was gone much of the time though not as far away from home. Still he was gone for long hours. Here in Washington he is often far away from home and that's very hard on families. That is what I sense is the biggest difference in living here.

Q. *Do these pressures ever get to you?*

A. Sure they do, and I miss him terribly when he's gone. There have been long separations this year because he is running for the Senate and he needs to spend more time back in the district. I'm just glad I'm a Christian. If I weren't, I don't know if I could cope with it. I really feel, though, that I'm a very strong person. I have had to face many difficulties in my life. I just know that being a Christian allows me to have dignity and a chance to know that life is going to continue and that we can be together in prayer which is the really big thing in our family.

Every morning the family meets at ten minutes to seven for prayer. If Bill is in Colorado, obviously he's not up at ten minutes before five! But I know that he prays for us every morning. Somehow this means a great deal to us. We can at least be together through prayer. But there are times when he's away . . . all the crises happen when Bill's in Colorado. The children are sick, the furnace goes out, or the car breaks down. And when I was terribly ill a couple of years ago and subsequently had my gall bladder removed, this really hurt Bill because he was away at the time. Sometimes I tell him on the phone of one of these crisis experiences, and he feels so badly that he can't be here when it happens. But you can't plan a crisis.

Q. *Having said all this, some of these things must get to you. You must have arguments once in awhile. You must go to him and say, "Look, five weekends in a row is enough, how about spending just one at home?"*

A. Cal, I don't do that. You may think I'm a real Pollyanna, but one thing I learned from a disastrous first marriage was that you just don't do that. I have worried about Bill, and I have wanted him to be home. I worry about his health. I used to worry about his smoking, this sort of thing. It does not help the situation any to get on him about it. I refuse to do it. That was part of my philosophy even before I became a Christian. I am not going to add to his burdens.

It's not that we don't share those things. I do go to him and say "Bill, it's been so long and what about the children?" and this sort of thing. But I do not gripe at him and complain to him about it. And I am not about to do it. It's a decision I made a long time ago and it works. That isn't to say that the feelings aren't there.

Q. *That's what I was getting at. How do you supress those* *feelings when they well up within you? Do you sometimes cry to get rid of your frustrations?*

A. No. I can't tell you when was the last time I cried. It's been years. It's because I have so much faith and confidence in Bill. We have always been able to talk about things. This was something I couldn't do in my first marriage. I think it surprised Bill when we had our first disagreement. I said, "Look, I can't stand this. I'm not going to have these long silences. We're not going to have you go your way angry and me go mine."

That's the way we started our marriage—and now we just don't argue and we don't fight. I don't think our children have ever heard us say a harsh word to each other. Bill is absolutely a woman's dream of what a husband should be.

I come from a background where the language is different, for one thing. I wasn't used to being treated so nicely. I have felt so special being married to him and it's not that I'm grateful and groveling at his feet. It's just that he has really made me realize that I am a worthy person. I knew that even before I became a Christian, although I must say that since then I've realized even more that God loves me—that I really am special. I never really ever felt all that special before, particularly during my teenage years and on into my twenties and thirties. I just have been extremely lucky to have found someone like Bill—and to be able to have the kind of marriage we have.

Q. *Obviously you don't look upon your role, your chosen role, as a wife the same way some feminists might look upon what you are saying. They might say that you're a doormat, that submission means slavery. You have your own identity. Who are you anyway?*

A. Well, first of all, I'm a child of God. Maybe I didn't used to see that, but now I do know who I am and I know where I'm going. I feel very secure about that. In the beginning I suppose I was a little in awe of Bill. And because our backgrounds are so different, perhaps I did really look up to him. However, over the years I've learned that I've taught him as much as he's taught me. There have been things he's been able to give me, but on the other hand there are things from my background that I've been able to bring to him.

Q. *For example. . . .*

A. Learning to relate to people. In our family we're farmers and we love everyone. We often just sit around the table and talk and laugh. When I see my brothers it's always a big hug and we're very close. Things like this I've been able to show Bill. It doesn't lessen or diminish a man to be able to show his emotions. And so we're very affectionate in front of the children. This is one of the neatest things. The first time Bill ever called me "honey" in public I just about died! It was the biggest thrill I think I've ever had. That just didn't happen in my former marriage. Anyhow, these things I think I've been able to bring to Bill: an openness and a warm relationship with other people.

Q. *If Bill wins the Senate seat, do you expect things to become more difficult—in terms of time anyway?*

A. I don't see it becoming any different. Bill is gone a great deal now. But we talked this out thoroughly before he ever made the decision to run for the Senate. We didn't really sit down and say, "This is the plus side and this is the minus side," but that's about what it amounted to. We could just as easily have chosen to go home, but we think there's a reason that Bill is here. We've given ourselves to Christ and we feel that we're leading Christ-centered lives. Our decision came through hours and hours of prayer. If we lose, that means we're not supposed to be here, so we'll cheerfully go home. We do want to win the election. We're not just sitting on our hands and saying, "O.K. God, take over," but I don't really see that our lives will be any different. Bill gives to his family as much as he possibly can. He always has and I think he always will.

Q. *How are you handling this campaign? Are you running against Senator Haskell or just for a seat in the Senate that happens to be occupied at the moment by him?*

A. Yes, we're running for an office, but you have to be realistic. There is someone in that office right now. As Christians we had to struggle with how you do that. Is it fair? Is it Christian? Is it what the Lord would have us do—to show the failings of someone else? We wrestled with that. And it isn't just for Bill and me. It's how you get this across to hundreds and literally thousands eventually—people who will be working on our campaign. We do not plan to deal in personalities or to dredge up personal facts about anyone in Mr. Haskell's campaign or himself. That's not our purpose. There are issues that we can examine and yet even in issues you wonder if you are supposed to hit hard. The only answer for us has been to pray about it. And that we do, daily.

Q. *Do you both pray for Senator Haskell? And how do you* *approach the issues and decide which you'll hit hard and which you won't?*

A. We don't pray for victory. We do want to win, however, or we wouldn't be in the race. But we don't make winning the point of our prayers. We do pray for Senator Haskell's safety, his well being. We pray that he, too, feels called upon to run a similar kind of race. And we pray for his staff and their safety. You know, safety becomes a big thing when you're away so much and travel the state as much as these people do.

I really can't speak for Bill but I do feel in my own mind that it is fair to point out the differences. That's what it's really all about. If the people have nothing to choose between then why get involved at all? Fortunately in this case it's very clear. Bill and Mr. Haskell operate from two different philosophies. So, unless the Lord tells us differently, that's the way we're going to handle it. No personalities. Just what he's done and how Bill would have done it differently and how he will do it if he's elected.

Q. *Do the Haskells know you are praying for them?*

A. I don't know. I doubt it. I don't think that it's important, necessarily, that they know, because that's so misunderstood. In the world of politics if you said something like that they'd think you were using it.

Q. *Tell me about how you became a Christian and was Bill a Christian when you married him?*

A. We thought we were. We belonged to a church. In fact, Bill joined my church. Bill was Presbyterian and I'm Lutheran, so he became a Lutheran. We worked very hard in the church. But it didn't seem to bring us real joy. Sometimes it became such a drudgery we'd rather stay home on Sunday morning to read the funnies—except we didn't! But you know when you attend church in that spirit there's no real joy in it. You have the feeling that you'd rather be someplace else. I surely would never mean to imply that the gospel was not taught at our church. It was. We just weren't listening. It fell on deaf ears, I guess. Not until we came to Washington did we find out what it really means to be a Christian.

First of all, I think it was through Fellowship House that I met a congressional wife who asked me to come to a Bible study with other congressional wives. When I went to it there was a little lady from Campus Crusade for Christ, Eleanor Paige, a really dynamic gal. She simply challenged my faith and I really thought, *Who does she think she is?* At first I was offended, because I had minored in religion at Denver University and had studied the various disciplines. I really thought I knew what it was all about. But she said something different: "When did you invite Christ into your life?" And I wondered what that meant. But I could not shake it.

I came home and that question bothered me all day long, washing dishes or making beds. *"When did you invite Christ into your life?"* I went back for the second meeting and she asked the same thing again. After the meeting I told her, "I don't know what you're talking about! What is a personal relationship with Christ?" Really through her, then, I came to realize what was missing in my life. I had some real problems but I was not able to solve them even though I tried. But nothing happened. There were bad habits and that sort of thing. After becoming a Christian, after asking Christ to take over my life, it still didn't happen overnight. But over the years I was able to calm down and see that those problems weren't as big as they seemed—and now they're gone!

All during that time I carried in my heart a prayer for Bill. He was watching, and we were still going to church. But it didn't appear to me that he really believed that what I was doing was anything more than just having fun. I loved the Bible studies. I'm a Bible study freak!

I'll never forget one Sunday, we went for a ride and I was just bubbling on and on, telling him things Eleanor had said, the wisdom she had been imparting to us as women. We drove up in front of our garage and parked. He didn't get right out, and so I asked him what was wrong. "Well, I'm not sure," he said, "but it seems to me you're spending an awful lot of time in Bible study and it bothers me." At that point I started to cry.

Q. *That was one of the few times you cried?*

A. Yes, about the last time. I said, "Well, I just won't talk to you about it any more." I was sure that what I was doing was right and that the decision I had made was right. It really hurt me to think he would disapprove. He said, "I don't disapprove. It's just that you're becoming the spiritual leader of this family and I know I should be—and I'm not." Well, that was the end of that conversation. I vowed inside that I would never speak to him again about my Bible study.

Q. *But wasn't that an incredible thing for him to say— realizing that he should be the spiritual leader but wasn't?*

"I don't believe in divorce"

A. He'd been thinking and watching and, of course, I couldn't keep quiet. Within two weeks I was back telling him all this stuff again. Maybe it was less than two weeks! Because we share and I can't imagine ever keeping anything from him.

A few months passed and it was shortly before Christmas a couple of years ago. When Bill spoke to me, his throat was very dry and scratchy. This is unusual for Bill because with his broadcasting background he has a rich, almost velvety voice. He said, "I think there's something you should know." I thought, *Oh dear.* I couldn't imagine what it would be. His voice was so different. And then he told me that he had prayed to receive Christ. He had been studying by himself and had also been working with a person from Campus Crusade. He had seen the gospel in a distilled form. . . .

Q. *The four spiritual laws?*

A. Yes, the four spiritual laws. He learned that he too could have this personal walk with Christ that I had. We hardly knew what to do with this new relationship. Even though we love each other very much and have a good relationship, this added a new dimension. I have found that our love for one another has deepened and we now stand and pray with our arms around each other as we start off our day. It's just so great to think that someone cares that much for you!

Q. *Getting back to your divorce for a moment. That's such a problem in Washington. Does anyone ever treat you with a holier-than-thou attitude? Is it a problem for you?*

A. No, I don't suppose that many people outside of our

Christian friends even know about it. It's certainly no secret, however. Yes, I wrestled with that before I became a Christian. Almost daily I would pray to be forgiven—for my part in the failure of my first marriage. This is one of the beautiful things about being a Christian. You only have to ask once to be forgiven and you are!

I don't believe in divorce. I was not a Christian at the time. And so the only thing I can do is ask to be forgiven, because I believe in God's promises and know that I have been forgiven. I go on from there. Now I find divorce inconceivable, not to say that there can't be problems in the future. It would be silly to assume that life is going to be just a bed of roses from now on. You work at these things daily. That's really the answer. If something were to happen, because we do love the Lord so much, we would be able to sit down and work on it from the Christian perspective.

Q. *Do you ever have any doubts or worries about your husband? He travels so much. There are so many women on the Hill and elsewhere who would be attracted to a congressman.*

A. No, I don't. I really don't. I'm not naive enough to believe that Bill couldn't meet someone else, because it does happen. But I don't worry about it. I see the girls on Capitol Hill, many of whom are much more attractive than I. If Bill wanted to have an affair, he could. But no, I don't worry about it.

Q. *Have you ever had any doubts about God?*

A. Yes, I did. At Denver University I minored in religion, as I mentioned. I believe most of my professors were atheists—which is interesting because it was a religion-philosophy department! I had certain beliefs. I believed what the Bible taught even way back then. But after going through these courses I really did wonder. Shortly before this time my marriage had failed. So I did wonder. I knew there was a force, something out there greater than I. But I surely didn't think there was anything personal about it.

Q. *How about now? You're grounded in your faith. Do you ever have problems with God, wondering if he's listening when a problem doesn't get a quick answer?*

A. No. Faith is such a simple thing. To me it's just the Word of God and his promises and then just believing. That's pretty simple. If you sit back and consider it, it's so overwhelming you think it can't be true. No, I have complete confidence in God.

Q. *And what about the future? If Bill becomes a senator, are there other goals to conquer? Vice President? President?*

A. No, not at all. I really only look at what he could do for the Lord being in the Senate. This is one of the things that made us decide. Not long ago in Colorado someone said, "You'd better cool it on this Christian stuff" and you know what Bill's answer was? He said, "It's more important to me to be a Christian than it is to be a senator." He wasn't pushing anything. It's just become known that Bill values being a Christian and he's willing to state it without apology. If we lose an election because of that, fine! Our real reason for being in Washington is to glorify Christ—not ourselves.

Billy Graham

Evangelist

In his sixtieth year at the time of this interview, Billy Graham continues to make his influence felt. Politicians, popular singers, fads have come and gone but despite criticism from some who don't share his faith and from some who do, "the greatest evangelist since Jesus," as *Texas Monthly* Magazine called him, preaches the same gospel he has preached since college days—and with as much effectiveness as ever.

Though I had seen Billy Graham on television and heard him on radio many times, I did not meet him until one Sunday morning in 1972. It was at one of those curious White House services President Nixon used to have. Graham was not preaching that morning. Much to my disappointment, he only led a prayer. I had always considered him a larger than life figure and as his deep, resonant voice boomed out over the specially invited audience (that included reporters such as myself who had been relegated to weekend duty) goose bumps dotted my flesh. The dynamism of that familiar North Carolina accent seemed even stronger in person than on television.

Later, at a reception for those who attended the service, I whispered to Graham that I, too, was a Christian and a news reporter. I hoped he didn't consider one the antithesis of the other.

"I am a shy person"

He shouted across the room for his wife, Ruth, to come
and meet me, advertising for all to hear that I was a Christian! It was my first, though unintentional, White House
"witnessing opportunity."

My first impression upon sitting down alone with Billy
Graham in his Montreat, North Carolina office, was of a
man who does not, as they say in the South, "put on airs."
He is a man who is gentle and humble, and he was there
to devote all of his attention to me. I had the feeling that
if I had been the gardener or the trash man, I would have
been treated with the same deference.

Anyone who has seen Billy Graham, whether on television, or in person, would come away feeling that here is a
man who must be on top of the world, full of self-confidence
and with few, if any, misgivings about himself.

I was amazed that that impression is inaccurate. . . .

Q. *One of Ruth's poems says, "Lord, when my soul is weary
and my heart is tired and sore and I have that failing
feeling that I can't take anymore. . . ."* In your humanness, do you ever feel like that? Do you ever wish,
just for a little while, that you could be an anonymous
someone else?*

A. I feel that way most of the time! The position I have
been thrust into by the media and others means I am
recognized almost instantly in airports and restaurants
and places like that. I'm sure this causes me to lead a
somewhat abnormal life, because basically I am a shy
person, though people would never guess it. But as I

---

* From *Sitting by My Laughing Fire* by Ruth Bell Graham (Word,
1977). Used by permission.

analyze myself, I think I am. I do not particularly like crowds and yet I'm forced to be involved in crowds. I love a small, intimate dinner party where I can go and listen and share with maybe four, five or six people. But a larger crowd than that is a bit difficult for me.

On the other hand, I don't suffer from depression because I can't be the private person I want to be. At least I don't think I do. And I wouldn't attribute that to faith in Christ, although certainly my faith is a basic element. When one has hope, you know. But I attribute this partially to the fact that by nature I am not a depressive person. Neither am I a person who lives on a big high all the time. Without question there have been highs and lows in my life but I've never had time to become unduly concerned. I've been too busy!

I spend anywhere from twelve to sixteen hours a day at work and that's seven days a week, except when

Billy Graham and Cal Thomas. *Ray Thomas photo*

I'm visiting members of my family. That's about the only relaxation I have. I had to give up golf—I used to play a lot of golf—because the pressure of my work had become too great. The older I get, the greater the pressure becomes. I don't know why that is. Or it may be that I had to slow down without being conscious of it. I'm thinking of taking up golf again because I think I need a hobby. Everyone needs a hobby. I wish I had one, but I don't. Or a sport. I don't play tennis. I've tried but I'm not good enough to play with some of the friends I'd like to play with. I do like to jog and swim. I do those for my exercise. Then I do calisthenics and things like that. But I love to study. Every hour I can I spend in study.

Now, as I look back, I wish I had spent less time speaking and more time studying. There are great areas of knowledge opening up to me now, even in theology, that I wish I had studied in greater depth.

Writing my book on the Holy Spirit* took more than three years. It was a tremendous revelation to me and a great help to me. I started out, not to write a book, but to study the subject for myself; to find out what the Bible really taught on the subject of the Holy Spirit. One of my problems was trying to reduce it to book size, because I had enough material to write a trilogy. In fact, my wife has been urging me to make it a trilogy, rather than just one book.

Q. *I believe that's what Carl Henry did on the inerrancy of Scripture.*

A. Yes, but he's a real theologian. I don't think anyone puts me in any classification like that, because basically,

---

* *The Holy Spirit* (Word, 1978).

I'm not an intellectual. Through the years studying has been rather difficult for me, but it's become a greater joy as I get older.

For example, I love to read historical novels. I've just finished one on Richelieu. That came as a result of a conversation with Charlton Heston. He said that the person he portrayed on the screen who took the most out of him was Richelieu. That came as a surprise to me because Charlton's played Moses and everyone you can think of. So I decided I was going to study the life of Richelieu. I read a history book on Richelieu and then I found a historical novel about him. I became fascinated with that period of French history.

Q. *Some of your close friends say you are the humblest man they have ever known. How does one stay humble in the midst of such notoriety, such exposure, such acclaim? Do you have to work at it?*

A. I don't know. I wouldn't agree with them to start with, because I never think about humility. It doesn't occur to me. I would not be able even to form an opinion or definition of humility. I wouldn't know whether I was humble or proud! I think there is rather a thin line between humility and pride.

I have to be totally dependent upon the Lord, because there are so many areas of my life, my work, and my ministry in which I don't have the ability to cope. I have to be dependent upon him physically because I've had so many little things go wrong through the years. If I had any tendency toward pride, I'm sure the Lord would take care of that as he did with Paul who had a thorn in the flesh.

Q. *Since Constantine there have been those in authority who have sought the support of the church or church leaders*

*to justify certain actions or inactions. You were under
pressure and some criticism during Vietnam and Watergate. Could you describe that pressure and the temptations you faced either to speak out or remain silent?
And do you think any of the criticism was justified?*

A. That's a difficult question to answer. I did speak out
quite early in the Watergate situation which, I think,
saved me from being tarred with it. I really knew nothing about it. I was not involved with the President or
his staff during the Watergate experience. But I wrote
for the *New York Times* Op-Ed page rather early on
Watergate and morality. I did not think at that time
that Mr. Nixon was personally involved or had any
knowledge of it.

Then I wrote a second article for the *New York Times*
Op-Ed page which they made a news article on the
front page. The reason I remember it so well was that
I was playing golf with Vice President Ford the day
it came out. Reporters were all over me around that
golf course, trying to get more comment. One of the
interesting people who wouldn't give up was Ron Nes-
sen. Then that night on the news I watched him. He
gave a wonderful explanation of why I kept saying "no
comment."

Q. *No wonder you gave up golf!*

A. But you asked about pressures. Especially during Vietnam I sensed pressures both ways and temptations both
ways. I saw the Vietnam experience in a little different
light than some because I had visited Vietnam a number
of times; I preached to the troops and in the churches.

And then I've traveled all over the world and I see wars going on elsewhere.

There are wars going on that we never even hear about! Take the war in the mountains of Columbia, South America. It's been going on now for about 25 years. Probably 30 to 40 thousand people have been killed. Americans don't even know about that war. Am I to go around the world and decide who's right and who's wrong in all these different wars?

Who's right and who's wrong in the Middle East? Who's right and who's wrong in the Ethiopian conflict? Those are just the ones we read about. Who really knows about the war going on between Vietnam and Cambodia? What causes lie behind it? Most people don't realize that those Montagnards are by and large Christians and will not accept rule from the Cambodians or the Vietnamese.

The Nagas are in revolt against the Indian government. Yet they don't want to be taken over by the Chinese, either. War is going on full-time there. And the Indian government wouldn't allow any European people in there for eight years. One *New York Times* man slipped in and got a story. I was the first one whom Mrs. Gandhi let in to preach at their 100th anniversary of Christianity. I found that 62 percent of the people of the whole state of Nagaland are Christians— Baptists. It's the largest concentration of Baptists in the world. And yet they're in a constant state of war.

Q. *At the same time there must have been people you respected who were raising a moral outcry saying, "O.K., I understand your feelings about other nations and other wars, but this is the United States of America. This is a country that has proclaimed concepts in its Constitution*

*and Declaration of Independence that no other country
in the world has even pretended to consider." Aren't we
called to a higher standard and as a person with influence, power, respect and recognition, weren't you getting
it from both sides as Senator Hatfield was?*

A. I got it from both sides, too. But I decided that I
wouldn't take a stand either way, and I never spoke
one way or the other on Vietnam. I would think if I
went through it again, I probably would take the same
stand, because there are too many issues like these that
come up. I've seen several presidents wrestle with Vietnam!

The first little involvement with Vietnam happened
under Eisenhower. Then when President Kennedy took
over he sent in 16,000 troops. When Mr. Johnson came
in the war escalated again, but the man who introduced
the Tonkin resolution was Senator Fulbright. The people who later became doves were hawks at an earlier
period. Everyone thought it was right at a certain point
in history—then it suddenly turned. And everyone was
supposed to be a dove. Many did a flip-flop on the
thing, because it became politically expedient to do so.
I didn't feel that I could do that. I just maintained
my neutral position on the whole matter.

Q. *I know better than to ask you to divulge what a president
said. You wouldn't anyway! But were you ever asked
by any of the presidents you mentioned or by a White
House staff person for advice or your opinion of the war?
Did anyone ask you, "Billy, do you think we're doing
the right thing?"*

A. Yes, I was asked. I went to Vietnam at Christmas and

Billy Graham

Cardinal Spellman and I stayed in the same place and had talks at that time. And when we returned, President Johnson invited both of us to the White House for lunch. Secretary of State Dean Rusk was there as well as (Walt) Rostow and McGeorge Bundy. Mr. Johnson turned to Cardinal Spellman and asked, "What do you say? What should we do?" The Cardinal told him what he thought we ought to do. His stance was hawkish.

Russ Busby photo

He turned to me and I said, "Mr. President, I'm going to limit my remarks to what I thought was the moral and spiritual condition of our troops and also to the moral and spiritual condition of the people as I felt it, saw it, and heard it through the lips of clergy and chaplains and so forth." And so I did not get to the aspect of whether he should do this or do that because I really didn't know.

Q. *In his autobiography of you, John Pollock says you have many temptations. Leaving what we've just talked about aside for a moment, what are some of them? And I'd like to touch on the lusts of the flesh, as President Carter did so openly in that famous* Playboy *interview. Have you had that problem? Or have you managed to isolate yourself from that by the personal rules you've set such as never being alone with a woman other than your wife?*

A. Well, I haven't had temptations in that way so much as some others might. I've never been strongly motivated in that direction. My wife and I have the most marvelously happy marriage possible. I would think that in my earlier years of travel, yes, there might have been temptations. But it never reached the point where I ever thought about one particular person or doing something.

For example, I had a clergy friend who was so strongly tempted in a Paris hotel that he had to lock the door and throw the key out the window! Well, I've never been tempted that strongly!

In the earlier years there were temptations, but I never let it get to the point where I was about to do anything. In fact, I'd asked God first of all in my own private commitment to kill me before I would ever yield to such temptation. I would rather die than compromise at those points.

Q. *What about some of the more subtle temptations?*

A. We're living in a period of great self-analyzation. I recently talked to a top psychiatrist who is a Christian. He said he believes some of the greatest problems he's encountering in psychiatry are people who are self-analyzing themselves. My son-in-law is a psychologist. He has said exactly the same thing. To try to analyze why one did this or that, he said, drives some people almost insane. And I've never been that type of self-analyzer. I've never sat down and analyzed myself so much.

I've known people who have destroyed their Christian usefulness by this self-analyzation. I suspect that we're all tempted in the same areas. I mean, we *are* human. Jesus was tempted in *all* points, yet without sin. I think we're tempted in all points—all of us at all times. That's the reason we're to wear the full armor of God—so that we can withstand the fiery darts of Satan.

There's another aspect I'd like to touch on. When you become visible, as I have become visible (and as many thousands are visible in these days of media penetration) the tendency is toward exaggeration. I suspect that those people in the limelight are not tempted any more than anyone else. But a Christian should take greater steps to protect himself and to be sure he doesn't yield to those temptations.

Q. *How have you done this? How have you taken these steps?*

A. I would think they are unconscious steps. For example, I never travel alone. I always have people with me. And the people who travel with me are people who treat me as an equal, not as their boss. Two of them are high school friends of mine (Grady and T. W. Wilson). They know how to kid me and, as they say, keep me humble. Whatever steps are taken are unconscious steps, but unconsciously I am constantly thinking, "Now will this compromise my faith? Will it bring glory to Christ? Or will this bring dishonor to Christ?" Those questions are in my mind all the time.

Q. *Then, of course, you have angels watching out for you!*

A. And I have angels watching over me, you bet!!

Q. *John Pollock also says that in the Boston Crusade nearly thirty years ago you unwittingly disobeyed the voice of God by not returning to extend the Boston engagement. Do you still discover incidents when you unwittingly disobey the voice of God?*

A. I don't know that I can point to any specifics, but I'm certain that I have disobeyed the Lord. In fact, I suspect that disobedience is a daily occurrence . . . a person I should have smiled at but I didn't. They're the sins of omission of which the Anglican Prayer Book speaks. Those are the great sins for which we're going to be held responsible. The things I should have done that I didn't do, as well as the things I did wrong.

I try not to sin deliberately. For example, I don't deliberately tell a lie. I'm sure I have told untruths, but I didn't think I was telling an untruth at the time.

Years ago many people thought evangelists exaggerated, so I told the people who handled our crusades to get the estimates of the crowd from the police, the committee or whoever was in authority. Then I instructed them to reduce it by ten to fifteen percent. We have maintained that wherever we've gone. As far as I can help it we never allow our people to exaggerate these things. Because we don't need to exaggerate. An old evangelist once advised me to claim ten thousand if everybody thought we had five thousand people. I left his office shocked that an evangelist would do or say such a thing. There's a matter of ethics involved in everything we do. Many times we've erred but we didn't just sit down and deliberately make a mistake— morally or ethically.

Q. *Do you ever lose your temper?*

A. That, too, is a difficult question. My wife claims she's never seen me lose my temper . . .

(At this point there is a knock on the door and T. W. Wilson enters with a grim look on his face. He says he has some very distressing news. Grady Wilson has just suffered a massive heart attack while on a visit to Manning, South Carolina.* He says it looks serious. Almost as if by reflex, Graham drops from his comfortable chair to one knee. His large hand grips the coffee table to steady himself. The other hand covers his eyes. T. W. also drops to his knees and I find myself doing the same thing in what appears to be the most natural of settings . . . three men, on their knees, praying to God in whom they all believe, for a man two of them have known all their lives and one has met twice. After Graham concludes the brief prayer, we all get up and Billy goes to the telephone where he attempts to contact a friend who has a jet plane that could fly Wilson to

---

* Following a long recuperation period, Grady Wilson was released from the hospital and is now on the mend. His travel schedule has been restricted by his doctors.

the Mayo Clinic. But Billy is advised Grady cannot be moved and so he asks T. W. to keep him advised and the interview resumes. Billy says he doesn't know how good a subject he'll be now that Grady occupies his mind. But he says he'll try. . . .)

Q. *You were in the middle of responding to my question about losing your temper . . .*

A. Well, as I said, my wife says she's never seen me lose my temper, but I think she's wrong. By. nature, I'm not a person who loses his temper. I didn't even before I was converted. You'd have to ask my friends about that.

Q. *What makes you angry? Even Jesus, as he was tempted in every way, expressed the entire range of emotions, even to the ultimate of sweating great drops of blood. He expressed anger. Other than being misquoted, what do you see that really makes something within you boil?*

A. There are times that I get irritated. Let's say when I lose a night's sleep and I'm very tired—tense and exhausted. I don't think other people detect it because one has learned to control it through the years. My wife could probably detect it, just by looking at my face, because she can read my mind! I get terribly upset at times over moral conditions in our country—the deterioration as I see it. I also become very disturbed at the deadness of certain churches and some of the theology expounded by certain clergy—or I should say lack of theology. And I get disturbed when I see men who are professed Christians with millions of dollars, dying and leaving nothing to the Lord's work. That disturbs me, because I know that they are going to go to heaven empty-handed.

Q. *Have you ever wanted something very badly and been denied it, not necessarily a material possession?*

A. No, because I've been offered so many opportunities: to go into motion pictures or to be an ambassador to a country or to serve in the Cabinet. The governor of this state called me back in the early '50s about accepting an appointment to the United State Senate. Three Senators in a row had died in a short time of heart attacks.

Then I have been urged to run for President several times by different groups. But none of those were really temptations. I couldn't call them temptations because I didn't even stop and think about them. I just said, "Lord, You have called me to preach the gospel and I'll never do anything else, so long as I live." I remember this is how I became close friends with Leonard H. Goldenson. He's Chairman of the Board of ABC. In 1949 or '50, Frank Freeman, who was president of Paramount, invited me to lunch. Cecil B. DeMille was there and several movie stars who were famous at the time— also Leonard H. Goldenson, whom I did not know. He was then legal counsel for Paramount. MGM, I believe it was, had signed Bron Clifford who was then an evangelist. It made headlines all over the country. I suppose other studios thought they should sign an evangelist, too, to counteract this publicity. They were going to pay him (Clifford) $50,000 a year, which was a gigantic sum at that time.

So I told the whole crowd that the Lord had called me to preach. I told them how I'd been converted, and I shared the gospel with them. Later when we had become very close friends, Mr. DeMille asked me to give him some suggestions on the making of "The Ten Commandments." He told me, "I'll never forget that day. I was really thrilled with your answer." And Leonard Goldenson told me the same thing.

So when Paramount had to divest themselves of their theatres, they made Leonard Goldenson head of the theatre chain. Then the theatre chain was able to get control of ABC for practically nothing—I think it was five million dollars. When I went on radio in the fall of 1950, it was Leonard Goldenson who put me on live. I've been on live over ABC radio ever since.

A year later, they asked me if I'd do a talk show live (on television) at eight o'clock every Sunday evening, which I did for three years. We have all the old kinescopes but I can't find anyone who ever saw it! Then we started our crusades live on television in 1957 at Madison Square Garden. And that was because of Leonard Goldenson. As far as I can remember, I never did give a second thought to any of these offers.

I received over two million telegrams in 1964, asking me to endorse Goldwater. It was planned, of course—an organized thing. And I told Mr. Nixon about it. He said, "Save 'em. They will be historic someday." I think they're bundled up in Minneapolis in big boxes. It took the telegraph office about three months to get them all to me.

I spent the weekend before the election with President Johnson. On my way home Monday afternoon, I was driving from Charlotte to Montreat. I heard the CBS newsman say that Billy Graham's daughter, Ann, had just endorsed Goldwater! Stopping at a pay telephone, I called Ruth and asked, "Ruth, what in the world is happening? You know we're staying out of politics."

She said, "I know, but Ann wanted to see what a political rally looked like, so she went down to Greenville and they led her up on the platform. She became so excited in the midst of all of it." Ann was only fifteen at the time, and they put the microphone in front of her.

So on Tuesday, the day of the election, President Johnson called and asked to speak to Ann. Since she was in school, he talked to me. He said, "You tell Ann she's a courageous girl and she's independent. Tell her that as soon as the election is over and you visit Washington again, I want you to bring her up here." He added, "I have an independent daughter, too."

Q. *People keep talking about "the next Billy Graham." You hear it everywhere. Is there going to be another Billy Graham? Should there be one?*

A. No, there will never be another because there will be someone far greater! I meet people on every continent who have far greater gifts than I have, far greater *evangelistic* gifts. God is raising them up right now. And I thank God for them. There are men who can just "preach circles" around me. I am not a great preacher, according to what some people call preaching. I don't have tremendous theological depth, as some people think. God has given me the gift of communication—communicating the gospel in a simple way. I am a communicator.

Now at this point in my life, I have to study to be simple, because otherwise my messages would get too involved. Working on my book about the Holy Spirit, I had to simplify it.

Q. *Any unreached goals in your life? Any prizes not won?*

"I feel totally inadequate"

A. No. My goal was to win as many souls to Christ as I could—to do all in my power to help evangelize the world. My goal in the early 1950s was to bring some visibility to evangelicalism. It was practically unknown for a whole generation in the '30s and '40s. In the late '20s, the whole evangelical position was ridiculed until the war came. Reinhold Niebuhr and others like him began to change this theological stance. They began to say, "There is such a thing as sin." Karl Barth and his neoorthodoxy began to change the thinking of other people. Then there came the election of Eisenhower, who I think made a profound impact on this country. He was baptized after he became President, and he joined a church. In his inaugural address he prayed, which was a shock to some people. We hadn't had that in a long time, if ever. All of this was happening about the time I came along. So it was two movements happening at the same time. Then I think *Christianity Today* made evangelicalism intellectually respectable. No other magazine at the time was doing that.

Q. *Paul spoke constantly of his inadequacies, his sinfulness, his weakness in the flesh. He wrote of wanting to do right but doing wrong sometimes, because of sin. What's it like when you feel weak? What do you struggle with that others could identify with?*

A. I feel everything Paul felt. For example, I've been asked, "How do you feel when you stand up to preach?" Usually I feel totally inadequate and wish that the floor would open up and let me drop through. There are many times when I stand up that I almost feel like running from the stadium. I feel like I have nothing to give these people.

Here are people who have come many miles (in some foreign countries they've *walked* many miles); they're expecting me to give them something to transform and change their lives. And then I remember that it's the power of the Word. It's not me. But I have this terrible feeling of weakness and inadequacy. Or maybe I've been going all day and I haven't had time to properly prepare my address.

On the other hand, there have been times that I've entered the pulpit extremely exhausted and left totally refreshed after about a thirty-five or forty-minute sermon. I used to preach an hour to an hour and a half. I've cut down now to about thirty-five minutes.

Q. *How will you know when it's time to slow down? I know you've slowed down some. But you've reached your sixtieth birthday. Some have suggested you might want to make greater use of the media to prolong your ministry.*

A. We're doing that this year. Not only are we running our crusades, but we're running specials this year. So many people are coming on television now with such tremendous backing. For many years I was the only one, certainly the only one in the evening in prime time. Now there are many. And I rejoice at every one of them.

One of the problems that we face and, I'm sure, many face, is this competition for the evangelical dollar. I will just not get up and plead for money, and so our income is down a little.

I'm no longer President of BGEA (The Billy Graham Evangelistic Association). I'm disassociating myself from the operational end of BGEA and its affiliates. Allan Emery has taken over that responsibility. I'm still chairman of the board, but I will move away from the organization more and more and just be a preacher and a writer.

Q. *That should prolong your strength.*

A. I hope so.

Q. *I know you've talked about death before. You've said you feel you won't be living much longer. What do you think about when you think of death?*

A. I'd be delighted to go today. I look forward to death. In a way, I suppose it's because I've studied a great deal in the Scriptures concerning heaven. I believe it's going to be something beyond anything we could imagine. Death is going to be a wonderful experience. I hope they don't dope me up. I want to experience death, because I think even the suffering of death is a part of life and that in suffering we gain spiritual strength.

I suppose part of it could be a form of psychological escapism. The pressures on me are great. By the time I was 60, I thought that I would have no invitations to hold meetings. But we have more invitations to the great cities of the world than ever before. We've had such a deluge of invitations to hold crusades in the most unexpected places: Bangkok, Singapore, every major city in India. We just finished four crusades in India. Our acceptance there was tremendous. And we've been invited to many parts of Africa—Zaire and Kenya—and all over Latin America. It's a world thing. I've spent two-thirds of the past six months outside the United States. Because I spend so much time outside of America I lose touch with daily happenings here. The foreign newspapers don't carry all the details of what is going on that one could read, let's say, in *The New York Times* or *The Washington Post.*

My schedule doesn't allow for emergencies. The older I get the more funerals I must attend. And it doesn't take into account a growing family. I have fourteen grandchildren. I never dreamed I'd want to be with my grandchildren as much as I did my children. I want to get to know them and to be a part of their lives.

Q. *Have you ever thought of what you'd like to say to Christ when you see him face to face?*

A. I know I'm going to fall down before him and say, "Lord, forgive me." I think that's what I'll say.

Q. *What would you like to be remembered for? How would you like to be remembered? Not with a statue or a plaque, I would think.*

A. If I had my choice, I would like to be remembered for bearing fruit. By that I mean love, joy, peace, long-suffering, gentleness, and so forth. I'm not talking about the spectacular gifts. There are twenty gifts of the Spirit listed in four places in the New Testament. Evangelism is one of those gifts. But I'd rather be remembered for fruit-bearing, because I think it's that person who lives it every day. The person who is bearing fruit probably is not conscious that he's bearing fruit. A person who is filled with the Holy Spirit may not be conscious that he is filled. Not one place in the New Testament did I find a person saying, "I am filled with the Holy Spirit." Not one place. It was said of others like Stephen being filled with the Spirit or Phillip being filled with the Spirit. But not once in the Bible did a person stand up and say, "I am filled with the Spirit." I think that people who are filled with the Spirit may be unconscious of it. And the same with people who are bearing fruit. I've met dear little old ladies and men in out-of-the-way places whom no one has ever heard of. Their names have never been mentioned in the newspaper. There's a man right near this house who spent most of his life in China. Almost ninety now, he's a giant among men. He did not have great gifts. He was not a great preacher—just a great man. He just bears the fruit of the Spirit. The Chinese knew it and his missionary associates knew it. Everyone who knows him, loves him— he wouldn't harm a fly. He's just one of those godly men. That's the way I'd like to be remembered.

Russ Busby photo

Jack Lousma

Astronaut

NASA photo

Jack Lousma was born forty-two years ago in Grand Rapids, Michigan.

Jack first wanted to be a businessman, but after attending business school for awhile, he lost interest and decided, instead, to study aeronautical engineering. He intended to go to work and avoid the draft by doing substitute military service in a defense-related industry.

A sudden compulsion, fed by movies he saw about airplanes, caused him to reconsider the military as a means of feeding that inner hunger to fly. He was too late for R.O.T.C. and the Naval Cadets wouldn't take him because he had just been married (at age twenty) to his wife, Gratia. Only the Marines offered him a chance and he grabbed it. It was to prove the best decision he ever made. It led to his becoming an astronaut and flying an important mission for the United States. (Skylab 2 with Alan Beau and Owen Garriott logged 1427 hours and 9 minutes in space from July 28–September 25, 1973). He was also back-up pilot for another one (Apollo-Soyuz with the Russians). This in turn led to his selection as one of the first astronauts to pilot the new space shuttle.

Jack and Gratia Lousma and their children live in Friendswood, Texas, which is situated nearly midway between Houston and Galveston. The town was founded by

Quakers, hence its name. The Lousmas attend the local Quaker church.

Jack Lousma is a perfectionist. His dedication to detail may be seen not only in his profession, but in the smallest things—such as making sure the barn door is closed and properly latched and the water hose is rolled up just right when he and his daughter feed and water the horses.

He is ruggedly handsome, a Marine's Marine. In a Charlton Heston look-alike contest, he'd easily win first place.

Q. *When did you feel right about getting into the astronaut corps?*

A. The first thing was to feel right about staying in the Marine Corps. I was about to get out and we prayed about it. I wanted to go back to graduate school—I was getting restless just being in the Marines. It seemed like I wanted to continually make progress in some direction or do something new. I don't know why, whether it was my ego, a desire for personal achievement, or what. It seems as if I thrive on that sort of thing and I really don't know why it is. So the Lord provided a way for me to go to graduate school and stay in the Marine Corps! That required me to spend more time in the service.

Then I grew restless again. After graduate school I went back to the reconaissance squadron, thinking that flying was a thing I wanted to do, but it seemed after I had learned to do reconaissance flying that the challenge wasn't there anymore. I began to get restless again. So I prayed that God would guide me and that he would make our ears open and our lives right so that we could hear his voice speaking. The opportunity came along to apply for the astronaut program in 1965 and I joined in 1966.

Q. *How did you first hear about the program?*

A. I first got word through the base newspaper. I answered an ad at the base in Cherry Point, North Carolina. The ad said, "Astronaut applications being accepted. Any Marine who wants to apply and meets these qualifications can do so." So I applied—and waited.

I applied and felt, "Well, I probably won't make this because I always thought they'd come after me instead of my going after them." But I filled out the application thinking I'd kick myself forever if I didn't at least try when I had the chance.

Immediately after that they sent me to Guantanamo Bay, Cuba, and I waited a whole month for the reply to come. I kept going into the administration tent and asking if the message was there. One day it finally came.

To make a long story short, I was selected. We moved to Houston with the distinct feeling this was what God wanted us to do. Since we've been here this same feeling of restlessness has come and gone and each time we've asked God to direct us, show us his will, give us a clear answer. Now we've received a definite yes, at least for one more trip.

Gratia has always been very supportive of me. She's never tried to rush me along or push me out or hold me back. We work as a team and I find it very important to include the family in the things I do. For this reason I feel that we've been able to maintain a good strong family relationship close to the Lord in spite of my high-powered and demanding job.

"I would like to have gone to the moon"

Q. *Did you ever have feelings during the period after you applied for the astronaut corps that you wouldn't make it?*

A. Initially I felt that I had an outside chance of being accepted. The odds were so great. I felt, *If God wants me there, he'll put me there.* If not, I hoped there would be something else on the horizon.

Every Marine aviator's ambition, I guess, is eventually to be the squadron skipper. I don't know if I had that ambition or not. I had always gone through life one day at a time. I never expected I'd be in this job when I was in school or in the Marine Corps, until I applied for it.

I never had a long range goal that I wanted to be the skipper or president of a corporation. One job would just follow another. Suddenly a light would dawn and I'd just follow it. And if that wasn't the right light, I'd get directed in a different direction. Eventually the Lord would put me where I needed to be. As I look back I can see that everything I did pointed me to what I'm doing right now. I don't know what I'll be doing tomorrow but I think I'm being prepared for that, too.

Q. *So when you faced frustration, how did you deal with it?*

A. When I first joined the program it was clear I wasn't going to fly right away. We were already in the Gemini program. There were a lot of astronauts ahead of me. Then we moved into the Apollo program and some of my contemporaries started to get picked up for assignments. I began to wonder when my chance would come.

Frankly, I became pretty frustrated because my chance didn't seem to come. So we prayed about this a lot.

Still, praying about it, in my opinion, doesn't take the concern away or the pain of worrying about it. It makes me know that I've done the best I can in talking to God about it, but still there is always this concern: *What if it's not in the plan for me to do this? I know there's a better plan for me but I'd sure like to know what it is, so I can ease my mind and start working on it.*

Whenever I feel restless, I don't feel it's right to sit down and wait for a blue light to hit me from above. I take definite steps that lead down to other doorways. In the most recent episode (of frustration while waiting for a flight), I pursued several other options to see what else might interest me, what else might be available—other areas in which God might want to place me.

I didn't fly very early with my group of guys. Up until I was selected I became very frustrated. But the flight was most gratifying, I don't know of a flight I would rather have been on. Of course, everyone would like to do everything. I would like to have gone to the moon. But I think God provided an excellent alternative and I think he has provided one now.

Q. *Does not going to the moon ever eat away at you? Was there a time when it did if it doesn't now?*

A. Yes. Some of my contemporaries were being assigned to flights to the moon. Now of my contemporaries, only three or four actually got to the moon so I really shouldn't feel disappointed. But I've always shot for the top. It's hard for me when I miss.

Q. *But did that gnaw away at you?*

A. Yes, it did. During the time when flights were going to the moon and I wasn't a part of the prime crew, I was working in the background and assisting where I could. But I felt that I was as prepared as anyone in my group to go. It did frustrate me.

Q. *Did you feel that you were better than some of those who did go?*

A. No. But I felt as if I were equal. I felt that some who went were better at that point in time and certainly were more qualified to go. . . .

Q. *Did you wonder about the motives of those doing the selecting?*

A. I didn't wonder too much about the motives. I did wonder about the selection process! But my mode of operation was always to work as hard as I could at the job I was doing and give it my best performance, thinking the next one for me was just around the corner. You have to realize that everyone else in the program is doing the same thing. We circulate among a bunch of high-powered guys, so I think the philosophy of those doing the selecting was that most everyone was qualified to do a good job and that's why it was tough to understand what selection process was used.

Q. *They never told you why someone was selected over you? Did you ever ask?*

A. No. It's sort of an unwritten rule (not to ask). To me it is. I prefer to work in that world by doing the best possible job I can. I know God has a plan for me. I would have been extremely disappointed had I never flown in space. But at this point if I never go into space again, that really won't shake the world for me. I just would want to know where it is I'm going to go next.

Q. *Marines are frequently perceived in the public mind as being strong-willed, never compromising and rugged. Did you ever doubt yourself and the direction you were going in the midst of your training and Marine career?*

A. I never had any doubts about the direction in which I was going when I was more active in the Marine Corps. Of course, I'm still on active duty. I've been in twenty years. In the astronaut program I had reservations about my relationship to the Marine Corps and my fellow Marines. Here I was a Marine, assigned to work at NASA and to fly in space. It didn't seem that I was accomplishing my objective. Meanwhile, my buddies were getting shot at in Vietnam. It seemed to me I wasn't really doing my part. So I did have some reservations. Before I was selected for my first flight, I wrestled very seriously with the idea of resigning from NASA and going back into the Marine Corps. I thought of going back in a squadron and flying and getting shot at like my friends. So this bothered me a great deal.

However, NASA always kept the carrot just a little out in front. Finally the carrot was taken. Now I'm glad that I did what I did. I feel that God was directing me at that point, too. Had I taken a leave of absence and then gone back to the astronaut program, I would probably have gone back to the end of the line and might not have flown yet. I guess patience was the lesson I had to learn—and I haven't learned it yet, frankly.

Q. *Have you ever had feelings of inadequacy, of self-doubt, of mid-career crisis creeping up on you?*

"I turned my priorities around"

A. I know I can't do this astronaut job forever. I feel I could do it for ten years yet. I'm forty-two. The question is will I, and do I want to? That I don't know. But I have wrestled with this problem, "Is it all worth it?" What I'm doing now is worth it. I came here to fly in space, not to do engineering work and related kinds of things. A certain amount of that knowledge is required in order to learn, but if I were to have to continue to work without the objective of space flight then I would probably go and do something else.

Since I left the backup crew for the Russian flight (Apollo-Soyuz) in 1975, I've been working on the space shuttle—but without any flight in mind because none was assigned until just recently. Frankly, that started to get rather old for me. I started asking myself, *What kind of progress am I making and what kind of challenges seem to be here?*

This period of doubt had its benefits, too. Because I had worked so hard on getting a space flight, flying in Skylab and then backing up the Russian flight, this had consumed all my time. I realized that for several years I hadn't done some of the things I ought to have been doing—like spending time with my family.

Fortunately, when I was doing this, the kids were small. Gratia was very much involved as a part of the program, so she was interested in what I was doing. The first time around it was worth it to her, too. But my kids are older now—they need me more. So I just turned my priorities around. I said, "Now the first priority is going to be family and the second is going to be professional." So since 1975 I've been able to pursue these priorities and keep them in the right order.

It's going to get a little busy again now, but still I think that from what I've learned in the past I'll be

Top: "Welcome Home" two days after splashdown—San Diego, 27 September 1973. NASA photo
Below: Astronaut Jack R. Lousma, his wife Gratia Kay, and their three children in 1972, l. to r., Matthew, 7; Mary, 4; and Timothy, 9. *NASA photo*

better able to keep the priorities a little more evenly balanced.

Q. *What's really so great about flying in space?*

A. *(Laughter).* For an astronaut or aviator who wants to go into space, the great part about it is accomplishing an objective.

Q. *Climbing a mountain because it's there.*

A. Right. And everyone has a different mountain. Flying in space was a challenge I wanted to meet to see if I could do it. Also, there's a little element of not only doing it, but surviving it. It's a gratifying feeling to get back on the ground and say, "I made it."

Q. *I've heard you talk about Yuri Gagarin, the Soviet cosmonaut who was the first man to orbit the earth. He said on his return that he'd been in space and hadn't seen God, therefore, there is no God. You went and came back and said you saw God everywhere. Because you have a different perspective, is it easier to see God in space than on earth?*

A. I was thinking about that in an airplane the other day. It's natural to look up when you leave the earth, whether you're in an airplane or a spacecraft. I think there's a kind of call to look toward God, but I don't think it should keep people down here from looking toward him as well. I have a much greater appreciation for the world God has made, the universe he's created. It's clear in my mind that this couldn't have happened by chance.

Q. *On Skylab, you were up with Al Bean and Owen Garriott. As a Christian who saw God everywhere in space, how did you relate this to them? Did you have any opportunities to express what you knew to be true?*

A. There probably were occasions I didn't use, but I think that is primarily because we had resolved all this on the ground before we went. Alan Bean is not a Christian, and Owen Garriott tends more toward atheism than anything else. We had conversations about this on the ground. Each knew how the other felt. So the kinds of things that might have been said up there had already been said down here. In my opinion it would have been nonproductive to continue in that vein up there.

I tried to maintain the same witness up there as I had on the ground. I conducted my own personal devotions before I went to sleep, reading my Bible up there. I took one along and they knew it. So I think I maintained the same consistency of relationship to God in their eyes as I did down below.

Q. *What was your favorite passage in space?*

A. The same as it is on the ground. Psalm 19 took on new meaning for me:

1 The heavens declare the glory of God; and the firmament sheweth his handiwork.
2 Day unto day uttereth speech, and night unto night sheweth knowledge.
3 There is no speech nor language, where their voice is not heard.
4 Their line is gone out through all the earth, and their words to the end of the world. In them hath he set a tabernacle for the sun,
5 Which is as a bridegroom coming out of his chamber, and rejoiceth as a strong man to run a race.

6 His going forth is from the end of the heaven, and his circuit unto the ends of it: and there is nothing hid from the heat thereof.

7 The law of the Lord is perfect, converting the soul: the testimony of the Lord is sure, making wise the simple.

8 The statutes of the Lord are right, rejoicing the heart: the commandment of the Lord is pure, enlightening the eyes.

9 The fear of the Lord is clean, enduring for ever: the judgments of the Lord are true and righteous altogether.

10 More to be desired are they than gold, yea, than much fine gold: sweeter also than honey and the honeycomb.

11 Moreover by them is thy servant warned: and in keeping of them there is great reward.

12 Who can understand his errors? cleanse thou me from secret faults.

13 Keep back thy servant also from presumptuous sins; let them not have dominion over me: then shall I be upright, and I shall be innocent from the great transgression.

14 Let the words of my mouth, and the meditation of my heart, be acceptable in thy sight, O Lord, my strength, and my redeemer.

Q. *If you had been the first man on the moon instead of Neil Armstrong, how do you think your life would have been different?*

A. If I had been the first man on the moon, I would have been pretty much the way I am now. I feel God has placed us in this environment for a reason. And he has given us many opportunities to witness for him, not only in a group, but on an individual basis.

Gratia has become a real shoulder to lean on for a lot of people. If I had been the first man on the moon, I would think that God had given me that opportunity for his purpose. I would make myself available for whatever use or opportunity that presented, just as I do now. I think that philosophy would not have been different.

If I had been the first man on the moon, there would

have been a lot more personal notoriety involved. This I really don't crave. In fact, the public relations aspect of the job, for me, has really worn off. I like opportunities to speak out for the Lord. I think that's the reason I'm here. And I like opportunities to speak up for the Marine Corps because I think that's why the Marine Corps put me here. But I don't relish going somewhere to make a speech and being patted on the back. Having people say, "Look at this great guy," doesn't turn me on. In fact I'd prefer not to do it. I like to be recognized professionally, as long as I've earned it. And that was part of the frustration I felt earlier. I had earned something that I wasn't getting and I wasn't being recognized for it.

Q. *At the beginning of the American space program, astronauts joined the more traditional heroes such as athletes, presidents and others. What's happened to our heroes?*

A. I've asked that same question. It's unfortunate. It seems that our society tries to pick a hole in a hero before he can become one. Maybe it's the great force of equalization that is such an undercurrent in our society today. You know we're going to make everyone equal, whether they are or not. If we have a guy who's starting to stand out, let's knock him down. I think there's some of that. It's hard to find a man who's head and shoulders above everyone else to be president. I don't know whether that's because there isn't a man out there who has the qualities that could make him into a hero. I don't know why it is—but I think I've touched on some of the elements.

It's more difficult to be a hero today because it's harder to stand out more as an individual. A person doesn't go on the moon or fly the shuttle himself, like a Charles Lindbergh. It takes a cast of thousands. And so the credit has to be spread around.

But God has his people in every walk of life and if they are doing what he wants them to do, that's what they ought to do whether they're astronauts or carpenters, teachers or journalists or whatever. And that's where they're going to shine best and be the most productive Christians.

Q. *When you prepared for Skylab, were you afraid that something might go wrong?*

A. There was a feeling that I might not go at first. Yes, there was a sense of personal danger—and I think that's one of the feelings that makes a person do this kind of thing. There's a certain amount of challenge involved in risk. You extend the thing you would least like to lose—your life—and if you can waltz off the whole scene with that intact, why that's the supreme accomplishment. That's why I'm here, I guess, in addition to wanting to serve the Lord where he has placed me.

Tom Landry

Head Coach of
the Dallas Cowboys

Coach Tom Landry at work. Player is wide receiver D. C. Nobles

What can be said about Tom Landry that hasn't already been said?

Landry is the only coach the Dallas Cowboys have ever had.

They started in 1960 with an expansion club some other clubs tried to keep from coming into existence. Landry began with a loser and built his team into a winner . . . a super winner. This team captured two Super Bowl trophies (1972 and 1978)—and just missed an unprecedented third.

Yet Tom Landry is different. He doesn't act or react or even dress like any other football coach. To look at him on the sidelines during a game, you wonder if he even perspires! He is so cool that CBS Sportscaster Pat Summerall once thought Landry's handling of a stick of gum significant enough to keep a camera on Landry and do a running commentary on it. The coach took the stick from his pocket, unwrapped it, put the gum in his mouth, and, instead of throwing the wrapper on the ground, he slipped it into his sport coat pocket to be used later to rewrap the gum when he was finished chewing it. That's cool!

I talked with Tom Landry over breakfast in Dallas at a restaurant next door to the Cowboys' offices on the North Central Expressway. It was the week before the NFL draft and he had a nine o'clock meeting with his coaching staff to discuss who would be selected from colleges around the country. The always gracious Landry tolerated the frequent interruptions of an SMU football coach hopeful in town for an interview. In addition there were a few friends and some autograph seekers ("this isn't for me, my boy wants it").

I'm a diehard Washington Redskins fan and the Cowboys are the Redskins' biggest rivals. I came away from the interview loving Tom Landry, but I still hope the Redskins beat them!

Q. *From what I've heard and read about you, probably the question you are most often asked is how do you manage to remain so cool on the sidelines in the midst of all that is going on? And how do you feel inside, particularly in a close game?*

A. During the game itself, I'm basically very cool, as you say. There are several reasons for it, but the prime reason is that I'm concentrating on my job at the time.

Most people don't realize that to perform well in whatever you do, especially in an athletic contest which is extremely emotional, concentration is the key. If you can keep your concentration, then you have a tremendous opportunity to perform at maximum efficiency. When you break your concentration, then you start to let other thoughts enter. So I'm constantly thinking about what's coming.

I'm never really conscious of what's going on at the moment, other than the mechanics of what we're doing on the field. For example, when I call a play, Roger (Staubach) executes it. While he does that I'm watching the point of attack. I'm trying to see what the blocking pattern is, to see whether or not the play is a good play or whether the defense has changed. That determines what I'm going to do in the future. I may appear to miss a great play. Dorsett may have broken for sixty yards, but I'm not really aware of his breaking at the time, because I'm watching the defense at work. This keeps me really concentrating. Most people, when they see a great play, tend to look down to see what kind of emotion I'm having. When they see me with no emotion they don't understand it. They don't understand why I'm not getting excited about the play they're excited about. That's the reason for it. I think this is the thing that seems to keep me unperturbed.

Another reason I stay cool is my Christian faith. Even in tough situations, it will keep me pretty level. Basically I know that football is not everything. At one time it was, as it is for a lot of people who haven't discovered the true meaning of life. God has a plan for me. Therefore, I'm not too concerned about whether we win or lose—or even whether I'm still the head coach of the Cowboys. I just believe it's God's plan and he expects me to do the best I can. These two factors, concentration and faith, are very important to the way I look and the way I act.

Q. *In Washington, D.C., where I come from, we had the George Allen philosophy for a long time. He told us winning was everything and losing was like death. He said the future is now. To some people, football has become almost a religion. Does that concern you?*

A. Whenever you become fanatical about something, that's unhealthy. However, I believe football today is a tremendous outlet for the emotions of people. I'm not a great believer in always showing things as they are—in the movies, for example . . . the rawness of life itself. I believe it's healthy to produce movies such as those I remember when I was growing up—where the hero won and everything ended happily. I believe people need that. Football is somewhat that way. People need an outlet for their emotions, something that gets them away from their problems, the things they're concerned about. I guess it's called escapism.

One of the biggest problems we have today in all professional sports is gambling. This causes people to react rather violently to the outcome of a game. For George (Allen) it may be that way. He's 100 percent football. There's nothing else in his life that I've seen.

I haven't personally dealt with George, therefore I don't know what's going on inside him. But after having competed against him for so many years, my reaction is that his statement is true. To him it *is* like death if he loses a football game. Therefore, it makes him a worthy opponent for me because it keeps me very much on my toes when I'm competing against him. But I think his attitude is wrong, because we know as Christians, there's only one purpose in life and that's a proper relationship with God. But there are people for whom God is not number one. For them their vocation or materialism are going to be the controlling factors of life. When your vocation or materialism becomes the controlling factor in life then one tends to do about anything he can to achieve "success." If he's not careful, he'll cut corners. Dishonesty comes into all types of business today because of this drive for "success."

Life is different for football coaches, as you know. It's a difficult life, because as soon as you lose, you get thrown out. That can have a serious effect on the family and every other relationship. Therefore, I can understand how some people who have football as the most important thing in life are going to do anything they can to win. I mean, that's understandable if it's your life.

Q. *You've been the only coach the Cowboys ever had. Some people would say that it's a lot easier to deal with temptation when you're successful and when you're winning. What are some of the pressures and temptations you've had to face on your way up to a winning record and being a coach in the Super Bowl?*

A. Back in those days when I first started, I had just become a Christian (in 1958) two years before I took over the Cowboys. I didn't know what Christianity really meant. I knew I was changed. I became a Christian during a Bible discussion. Though I'd been a churchgoer all my life, my priority had been football. Through that experience in the Bible study I accepted Christ. In those early years I was just a young Christian and I really didn't fully understand what it was all about. Oh, I knew what the gospel was. I'm talking about the effect of Christ upon one's life.

I had great confidence in the coaching area. If it hadn't been for the owners I had, however, I probably would have been fired. We were zero and one the first year, I remember. Maybe we won two or three games the next year. I think four was our high season and the next year we went down to three. That's about the time you change coaches in football. So I was that close to losing my job—but I really wasn't aware of it. Since that time I have observed many coaches who have faced similar situations. They've been fired and I've seen the effect it had on their personalities. But I haven't really experienced that.

I've been very fortunate to work for the ownership we have had. I signed a new ten-year contract at that one low point in my career, in that fourth year. Mr. Murchison* is the kind of a person who sticks with you, if he believes you have the ability. So that was a tremendous experience for me as I look back on it.

I felt pretty low in those years because things weren't moving very fast for us. We were the first expansion team in the National Football League, so we had no draft the first year. We just started out with nothing—really struggling. I think all athletes struggle with ego. Pride and ego are tremendous components of success—especially in a sport that is as competitive and physical as football is. You have to be psyched up, you must have that type of motivation going for you. So I guess the thing I've struggled with most is ego. Even after committing my life to Christ, which is basically giving over my will and making him the center of my life, I haven't found that it comes easy. I wish it did. But I think I've struggled with that problem more than anything else.

I test myself when I'm enjoying success and basking in the plaudits of people. I think it's human nature when that happens to you. And I know that it's wrong, basically, for a Christian to feel that way. So I guess that's one of my basic struggles most of the time since I've been a Christian.

Q. *Do you struggle with it now even more with two Super Bowl victories, all of the television exposure?*

A. No, no struggle. I've been able to overcome it to some extent. Yes, I enjoy it. It's exciting to be carried off the field at the Super Bowl. I'd be foolish to say that it wasn't.

---

*Mr. Clint Murchison, owner of the Dallas Cowboys.

Q. *And why shouldn't it be?*

A. But I really don't get carried away with it. You know, I don't feel any more that ego is one of my basic problems.

Q. *What are you struggling with now?*

A. I guess the biggest thing that I struggle with is fulfilling God's will, especially in the position in which he's placed me.

When you're the coach of a Super Bowl team, the demands upon you are tremendous. The demands upon me as a Christian are tremendous. Churches all over this country, Christian businessmen's clubs and women's clubs . . . I mean a day just doesn't go by but what I get a number of invitations to speak some place. And where is the dividing line between family and your service to God? I struggle with this all the time.

Sometimes I turn them down. I think, *Well, I need to have some time off.* Then I feel guilty because I haven't gone some place where I feel I might have been a good witness. Actually my off season is as difficult as my on season, just because of the speaking engagements. And there are eight or nine coaches I need to guide and direct during the off season and planning for the coming year. I feel guilty at times because I haven't done my homework so I can help these men move forward in their jobs. To me this is a constant struggle.

And then, at home, my wife suffers from July till January with me working seven days a week. There's no time at all, except for football. Then off season she expects more time and yet my calling to serve God is great, so I guess everyone has that struggle.

"I don't try to dictate"

Q. Sojourners, *a Christian magazine that is considered liberal by some, had an article called "Born Again Broncos and Converted Cowboys." The author, Wes Michaelson, talked about the last Super Bowl game and he said, "It epitomized competitiveness, brutality, commercialism, and sex." Do you accept that indictment?*

A. Well, like any view of life, it just depends which end of the spectrum you're on. Those who compete in football, and I can only speak for the Cowboys, don't see it as violence. But I can understand how someone viewing it from the other end could see it that way.

I don't think football is a violent sport. It's a sport that's very competitive, very aggressive. You have to be in top condition to perform it. If our players weren't working right now during the off-season program, they could never take the punishment. So from that point it could seem violent if you're not prepared, because there are injuries and other situations—fights on the field and so on.

Yes, sex can be a problem . . . the sex symbol. I don't have any control as far as the cheerleaders are concerned. I don't approve of them, personally, but that's not my area. No one within our organization tells me how to coach—and I don't get involved in these other areas. They know how I feel about it (the cheerleaders).

Q. *What have you said about the Dallas Cowboys Cheerleaders?*

A. I just felt they shouldn't be overexposed. They look like a chorus line instead of cheerleaders. I don't feel that it does anything for football at all. But the other half of the organization doesn't feel that way, which I

accept. I try to influence it where I can, but I don't
try to dictate.

Q. *Many people struggle with this problem in business and
other areas. They may be Christians who really love the
Lord and want to serve him. But they see things in their
line of work that are contrary to God's will. At the same
time one can be such a strong witness that he winds
up getting fired. So where do you personally draw the
line?*

A. I believe it's wrong not to allow your Christian beliefs
to affect everything you do. Reporters say to me, "Give
me an example of how you're a Christian." Of course,
as you know, once you become a Christian then your
life should revolve around Christ. Everything you do
reflects what you are. Therefore, if your life doesn't
reflect Christ, then it's questionable whether you're a
Christian or not. James says it's by works that others
will know about your faith. Paul looks at it from the
other end. He says you must have faith first—and that
works will follow. Both are correct. Either way, I believe
that one must speak out.

Now if it ever came to a confrontation between my
coaching the Cowboys or defending what I believe is
right, then I would defend what's right. And I wouldn't
be coach of the Cowboys anymore.

When I took over the Cowboys I had the basic responsibility of handling the football team. Everything that
has to do with the football team is my responsibility.
I've never been forced to do anything different in eigh-
teen years. The other area belongs to someone else.
So I might say to the one in charge of other aspects,
"I don't think that's right." However, it's his job to

say whether it continues. Because I am a Christian, I get letters all the time from people who ask, "How can you be a Christian and have that type of exposure on the sidelines?" I can only answer as I just have. I believe that Jesus walked with sinners and handled the situation.

Q. *Is God interested in football?*

A. I think God cares about everything we do, down to the smallest thing. He's interested in what's going on out there. I think we must be very careful not to expect God to intercede for us. We have this problem some-times, particularly with those who are new to Christian-ity. They feel that because they became Christians they must be winners. This is a very ticklish situation. Do you pray to win—or what do you pray about? I do feel that Christians are better athletes because they are Christians. Now that doesn't basically mean that God is helping them win. Most people don't fulfill their po-tential because of their own fears and anxieties and the doubts in their minds. I believe the great calling for the Christian is to use the talents God has given him to the best of his ability, at whatever level that might be. And I believe that a Christian athlete does become a better athlete just because of that. He knows his life is in God's hands and that he's able to fulfill his talents.

That's the sense in which a Christian athlete becomes better. It doesn't guarantee winning, because I don't believe God intercedes in that way. He could if he wanted to. He could do whatever he wanted to! Before we go on the field our prayer is that God will let us use our talent to the best of our abilities. We want to play the best that we can. We pray to be protected from injury. We pray this for the other team as well. This is our basic prayer every week.

Q. *In your football career can you ever recall having prayed to win a game?*

A. I can't say that I didn't. I'm sure I've been able to rationalize praying in that direction. It comes from the idea that we ought to win—and that it's really important for us to win as far as our team, itself, is concerned. In those situations I probably have in the past prayed to win. I've prayed not just to win the football game, but for the effect it will have on the football team. We may be at the point where a victory or defeat can change the complete complexion of a team, which most people don't realize. Unlike baseball which has 162 games, football may ride on one or two games—and even one or two plays can change your whole outlook. So it is possible that I have prayed to win. I'm not really conscious of it, though.

Q. *Do you ever pray for something and feel you haven't received an answer?*

A. Well, sometimes I think I should get a "yes" reply quicker! I've learned that when you pray God will answer your prayers. He doesn't always give you what you want—and that's the hardest thing to see. When we pray we see things in a different light. I've learned a great deal from prayer. At first, I was bothered because I thought I didn't pray very well. I'm still not sure that I pray very well. I guess everyone has that problem to some extent.

I'm not concerned anymore about how God answers prayer, however. I just feel that he is going to answer.

The answer may not be to my liking—but I know he is going to answer my prayer in some way. His own way.

I've seen God answer prayer, especially when I'm "down." Some years ago we had some struggles with the Packers. A couple of times they had great teams—and we almost beat them. We came back the next couple of years to go into the playoffs. Then Cleveland beat us very badly when we were supposed to win. After games like those—it's a struggle! It really hurts to lose games like that.

Q. *Losing games . . . is that the only thing that gets you down these days? Do you ever find yourself depressed for no reason at all?*

A. I was sharing with you about the off season, trying to fulfill all the obligations. Sometimes I get depressed then. I just have to stop and have a quiet time and really get my mind straightened out. But that's the only thing that really seems to get me depressed any more, other than defeat. Defeat doesn't bother me if I really felt that I've done my best. It hurts when I feel we could have done better. I always feel responsible as a coach whenever our team doesn't perform well.

In those years I was talking about, in '68 and '69 when we were badly beaten in the playoffs, the thing that amazed me was that I couldn't sleep at night. I was completely down. But then, as I asked Christ to strengthen me it was just amazing how, within a couple of days, I was back with renewed vigor. Only God can do that. I can't. I don't think that anyone can pull himself up off the floor by his own strength in that situation.

The Coach Landry the crowds see

"Winning is not my driving ambition"

Q. *Any unreached goals? In the sports world, you're on top. You have money, success, notoriety, fame. You have everything that many non-Christians pursue all their lives and never get. One would think there'd be no mountain left for you to climb.*

A. I believe that coaching is something I'll do as long as I enjoy working with players and seeing them develop— seeing them do the job they need to do. When I lose that joy, then God has something else for me to do. So I really don't get to feel as though, "I've got to do this; I haven't done that." I've never had goals to be a Super Bowl champion, other than a team goal. I'm talking about my own goals, my own personal drive.

Sometimes, I'm amazed we're as successful as we are. I look up and ask, "How did we accomplish all this?" But I don't have such goals.

If we had won the Super Bowl we'd have been the first team ever to win three.* I mean, those are great goals. But it takes years and years of background ever to get in the position to achieve them. Winning is not my driving ambition. That's our team goal, our normal goal-setting process. But I'm not driven by it. I didn't die because we lost the Super Bowl this year. Losing isn't like death, as George Allen says. It really isn't. And he'll discover some day that it isn't. Living for Christ each day as he gives it—that's what it's all about.

---

*Dallas lost to Pittsburgh, 35–31, in Super Bowl XIII. Pittsburgh thus became the first team to win three Super Bowls.

George Thomas

Speaker
British House of Commons

The Home Missions Handbook published by the Evangelical Alliance says Britain is becoming less Christian because of declining membership in the church and the increasing strength of other religious bodies.

Part of the reason for the "decline" is immigration. Large numbers of persons following the Islamic faith are coming to Britain. Another part of the reason is the encroachment of secular humanism and materialism which are gaining a tighter grip on all of Western society.

Standing faithfully against this rising tide is the Speaker of the British House of Commons, George Thomas.

George Thomas was born seventy years ago, the son of a miner from a valley community in South Wales. He grew up in that mining town during a period of severe unemployment and great hardship as well as social injustice.

Thomas is an unusual politician in many ways. He grew up poor. Most of his friends and associates were poor. He had no influential friends and yet, he says, he considers himself a very fortunate man.

He attended the state normal school with others in his neighborhood and managed to win a scholarship to the grammar school, an honor of which he is still proud. From there, he attended University College, Southampton, where he studied to become a teacher. After graduation he taught for awhile at the East End in London, but he was soon able to get employment in a town only twenty miles from his home in South Wales. That job helped him contribute to the meager family income.

Thomas was reared in a home with two brothers and two sisters, himself in the middle. He is the only one still living ("They're all in heaven waiting for me. Well, somebody must be last!").

He never married ("but I had what I call 'narrow escapes' "). His life has been mostly politics, but politics with a base that is grounded in God with whom he has had a relationship for most of his life.

George Thomas was interviewed by my friend and fellow journalist, Andrew Quicke, in the Speaker's House, overlooking the Thames River which flows past the House of Commons and the House of Lords. The British call it the Palace of Westminster.

Q. *When did you first become involved with the Labor Party?*

A. In my early teens when people thought the only hope for escape from the misery in which they found themselves was through the House of Commons. Democracy is in the blood of our people and they believe we must use a political weapon to create a new society. And I've lived long enough to see it created. The grinding poverty no longer exists in this country. Our welfare state is much criticized by the wealthy, but not by the poor. That has been for me an expression of Christian belief in the brotherhood of man, translated into legislative terms.

Q. *You came up through the political ranks the hard way,* *as a worker. You were never actually a miner, were you? You were a teacher, but you knew mining families.*

A. My brother was a miner. My father was a miner. All my friends worked down in the pit, so I felt a part of the mining community.

Q. *Did the coal dust, the terrible working conditions, and the oppression—I'm thinking of the strikes and lockouts in the early days of this century—did they cloud your vision of God and the vision of God for your brothers and the rest of the family?*

A. Oh, never. It was the vision of God that kept people alive, that kept them going. They worked under such terrible conditions. The lungs of the men who worked in the dust of the coal mines have been permanently affected. It was only through religion that they found any inspiration at all.

Hymn singing came naturally and I believe it was true in my generation as it was in Wesley's—it was only Christian faith that kept us from many bloody civil troubles in this land. There's no doubt we had the extremes of wealth and poverty, which provoked people when they saw their children hungry and knew that others had more than enough. Naturally some wanted to resort to desperate measures. But our faith kept us on an even keel and encouraged us to use the democratic process to fight for improvement in living standards.

Q. *Do you see God's hand in your elevation to the position of Speaker and to what end, for what purpose?*

"I'm an optimist about the future"

A. I do see the hand of God in my life. When I was in my teens, I felt a call to the Methodist ministry. I was convinced of it. But I remember my mother saying, "If you are, George, God will find a way of making it possible for you."

When the door didn't open and I became a teacher, I thought, *I was wrong.* But as I looked back I can see that my sense of call was right. I was called into the ministry, but my ministry was to be in public life. As you know, I'm still a local preacher with the Methodist church and I have felt that God has guided me in that calling. Certainly, I remind myself every day in this House where we are now that God has led me here. I look to him for wisdom and strength, for the patience, the humor, the gifts that are necessary for the job. But I do believe that God has led me as he leads everyone who is willing to be led. But it's up to me to make the most of the opportunity that has come my way.

Q. *What is your greatest source of frustration as a Christian and as a politician in the role of Speaker, particularly in view of what we hear about churches closing in England and people talking about faith on the wane?*

A. I don't believe that faith is on the wane. In fact, I think there are signs that faith is increasing. We've been through a difficult decade and a half where the emphasis has all been on materialism, on the acquisitive society.

I don't say we've escaped the results of this because the evidence is all around us. The acquisitive society is a very real force in our world. People think they have the right to put themselves first and never mind the impact on the community. But a large number of young people are rebelling against the influence of television and the media in general. They're looking for something more substantial in life. So, I feel encouraged, because I'm an optimist about the future. I think that the quality of our young people is as good as it has been in British history—and certainly as good as it is in any other country in the world.

Q. *Can you tell me about temptation, political compromise, and how you approach that consistent with your system of values?*

A. The demand for compromise doesn't come as much to the Speaker as it does to those who are serving in the battle, in the House of Commons Chamber. But I was there and I went through three decades serving as a partisan. Of course, there were times when I went through agonies of doubt.

I've watched strong men on both sides in this House going through torment with their consciences because they wanted to do the right thing. But they had a party loyalty as well. They'd been sent here because of that party loyalty. That has to be remembered. A man is breaking faith with those who sent him here if he deliberately goes back or changes his mind on the things that he stood for when he was elected.

Sometimes I've landed in trouble because I've been out of step with the party. Not often, because it's in the nature of people to join the party which represents their basic beliefs. Ninety-nine percent of the time you will agree. Take the Transport Policy. There's no crisis of conscience in this. It's a matter of how do we best serve the country—by a publicly owned system or a privately owned system? We're going to be debating that all day today in the House of Commons.

I don't think there's any more difficulty for a man in politics to be true to his conscience than there is in business and commerce and the other walks of life. People in other jobs are so quick to criticize politicians. They seem to forget they have a beam that would reach from here to New York in their own eye! A little Welsh exaggeration! But, after all, politicians are human beings. They are representatives and they try to find a middle ground on which they can reflect the views of those they represent, while at the same time being true to themselves.

My own experience is that most politicians will be true to themselves and then face their constituents and see what happens. My further experience is that constituents much prefer a man to be true to his own convictions—even when they don't share them. They don't withhold support because a man has voted for something they don't want—but they are likely to withhold support if they think a man is insincere and just playing up to them.

Q. *Do you have chances to share Christ with your colleagues and others in the government? And how do you go about that?*

A. As it happens, this very morning twenty of my colleagues were here for a prayer breakfast. We had a reading from the Scripture and prayer. Then we talked about colleagues who are going through a difficult time just now with family sickness. Some are sick themselves, and some are bereaved. We meet once a month and our group is across the board politically. People from all parties come in. We don't want any impression abroad that there's a sort of free masonry among those who happen to have Christian convictions. I'm afraid that those who belong to our group may often wonder why I don't give them any priority. This is one of my difficulties.

The frustration of being Speaker is, of course, that I cannot comment on controversial issues. They're the only issues worth commenting on! Who wants to talk about something on which everyone agrees? It's the controversial areas where we need to take a stand! However, I've been here long enough that others know my views—and they know when I'm counting up to 10,000 in the Speaker's chair, because I can't join in myself.

In the United Kingdom the Speaker is very different from any other country in the world, because he's far more nonpartisan. In this House, unlike the rest of the old Commonwealth or the new Commonwealth, the Speaker has to withdraw from his party and remain completely outside. This is a big price to pay when one has given a lifetime of loyalty to a cause that he loves. But it is surprising how Speaker after Speaker (once he dresses in his wig and gown in this House) assumes the responsibilities and the loyalties of his predecessors. You see their pictures around my wall? Sometimes I say I'm like the Chinese. I worship my ancestors. But I don't, really. I court my predecessors very much because this House is guided by precedent.

Q. *As Speaker you've had to face some pretty difficult decisions during this last session. Do you anticipate the pressure keeping up?*

A. Yes, I do. The clerk of this House, my chief adviser, said to me last week, "There's not been such a difficult Parliament since 1909." I have had to make major decisions on new issues where there was no precedent, but that's part of the challenge of the job.

We've now started broadcasting our proceedings. It's having a devastating effect on the life of the House, itself, because we're in a runup period before the general election and everyone who is there is a politician. I can't blame them for wanting to use the microphone to speak to millions outside in a way that they couldn't do before. That has brought a new dimension into our parliamentary affairs. After the general election, whenever it comes, this year, next year, I'm hoping we'll just settle down and behave as we did before we had the microphones.

Q. *What about constitutional battles between the House of Commons and the House of Lords?*

A. Well, we had an interesting battle recently which had no publicity, because it happened late at night. The Lords had deliberately passed two amendments which increased taxation. They had no business at all passing such resolutions. So when these amendments came down I advised the House not even to discuss them, but to turn them down and send them back with this message: This House is responsible for any resolutions dealing with taxation. I am pleased to say the Lords accepted it! And I heard no more about it.

Q. *Dr. Francis Schaeffer has talked about the need for Christians to make an impact with the biblical value system on the world. He also says there must either be a return to the Christian consensus of absolutes and moral values, whether or not everyone is a Christian, or there will be authoritarian government to control the chaos that results from the absence of such a value system. Do you see things as clear-cut as this? And how does a political person go about accomplishing this sort of goal?*

A. First of all, it is sobering to realize that at this time there are only twenty-five democracies left in this world. By a democracy, I mean those countries where there is more than one political party, where there's an alternative government under an alternative party, ready to take over responsibility as a choice for the people.

Secondly, I believe there is a link between what people believe and how they behave. Even in our own country with its rich history, if we throw out the standards that guided our fathers, then we are embarking on a very dangerous course. I do believe that people can be good without having Christian convictions. I've seen too many of them not to know that. Many people who do not make professions of Christian faith live superb lives of service to their neighbors. Having said that, however, I must add that I believe God has spoken to the world through Christ. He has shown us how to live. To ignore that message is the route of foolishness. I think that what the learned Doctor (Schaeffer) is saying has a germ of truth in it, but I don't agree with everything he says.

Q. *Looking forward, now, when this Parliament ends, will they reelect the Speaker?*

A. In this country, once a man is elected Speaker, it doesn't matter which party comes in. For over 200 years they have always reelected the Speaker. It is the decision of the House, however. No one has the right to assume that he will be reelected. I'm in the happy position that whether they reelect me or not, it doesn't cause me any worry. One can only be a good Speaker if he's independent and not worried about the future. And I'm not worried. God has led me so far and I'm sure he will lead me to the end of the journey. I'm much too near the Great Divide to allow my priorities to go wrong now.

Q. *George, do you ever get depressed and, if so, what about?*

A. That's not an easy question. I'm rarely depressed. About a month ago I did find I was wrong about a certain matter. There had been some trouble in the House. But a good night's rest got me over it and I thought, *Well, the only thing to do is to be right the next time.* We're all frail human beings and the man who doesn't make mistakes hasn't been born—except for our Lord! At least I haven't met anyone yet who has never made a mistake.

I think that if I always walk in the consciousness that God is with me, as he is with us now, and talk with him as I do every day, many times a day, it's very hard to get depressed. I believe in God's love and in his power. I've gone through some terrible times and shuddering experiences with bereavement . . . but our Lord shed tears of bereavement, too. However, I've bled because I've had my share of sorrows. Still I've learned that one is given strength in strange ways if his trust is complete. Then he will never be left alone. So, depression, so far, has not been a problem for me.

I like people. I think that every person has some good in him. Some of my colleagues would be quite surprised to hear that! But I really believe that if we treat people in terms of their possibilities, knowing what they could do by the grace of God, then our own lives will be made a lot easier and sweeter. This is the way I seek to live my life.

Johnny Cash

Country Music Singer

Johnny Cash

Johnny Cash. Just say the name and no further words are required. He has been a country and western singing star for the last twenty-three years. He turns even the most sophisticated concertgoer into a foot-stomping, whistling, whooping participant.

What kind of man is the real Johnny Cash? What is he like offstage, minus the lights and sound system? Without the adulation of the thousands who come to see him in person and the millions who have heard and seen him vicariously through his records and television appearances, who is Johnny Cash?

The first thing you find out about Johnny is that he's hard to reach. He's rarely in one place long enough to receive messages. Even his secretary, Irene Gibbs, in Hendersonville, Tennessee, has been stood up on more than one occasion when he promised to come to the office to take care of business. He is in perpetual motion, a nervous man. If you didn't know better, you might think he was running from the law or pursuing a dream!

It took seven months of letter-writing and phone calls to get an appointment with Johnny. At that time we were able to sit down and talk about his innermost feelings.

It was an August night in Washington D.C. Hot and muggy, it was the kind of night that makes your shirt cling to your body and the crease in your trousers disappear.

Wolf Trap Farm Park is a beautiful entertainment resort, nestled in a wooded area in the Washington suburb of Vienna, Virginia.

Backstage, flies battle one another for the privilege of biting the stage hands. Over in "Polly's Corner," business is slow. Two signs tell you paper cups cost two cents each. A park ranger (Wolf Trap is operated by the National Park Service) comes in and orders a ham and cheese on rye. A stage hand is overheard talking about what a man of God Johnny Cash is. It is not meant to be a compliment. There is laughter.

Through a set of double doors is an area that looks like a locker room without players. A large wooden cabinet partially obscures another set of double doors. "Do Not Enter" has been scrawled on the cabinet.

I walk into the forbidden room dotted with naugahyde couches and chairs. Almost on cue through another door that leads to the stage strides the man in black. He sees me and asks, "Who are you? Do we have an appointment?"

The eyes of partially painted ladies shift from mirrors rimmed in lights to the two of us.

"Yes, Johnny," I say bravely. "I'm Cal Thomas and your agent arranged this time for me to interview you for a book I'm writing."

He smiles, walks over, and extends his hand. It is one of the largest hands I have ever seen. His hand grips mine tightly, but not so as to impress me with his strength. We sink into the naugahyde with a whoosh.

Johnny Cash looks every bit of his forty-six years. But he is a beautiful forty-six (later on stage he breaks up the audience by saying, "A lot of people in the business as long as I've been say they still feel like they're twenty-five. I don't. I feel like I'm forty-six!").

His face seems to have been chiseled out of a stone. It

is not to be looked at so much as it is to be studied. Each line tells a story.

The son of an Arkansas cotton farmer, Cash has become the biggest thing to hit country music since they started recording it over fifty years ago. His appeal transcends economic, social, and racial barriers. His crowds are enthusiastic whether they assemble in glamorous theatres, at racetracks or in prison yards.

If Elvis was the king of rock and roll (and the two started together at Sun records), then Johnny Cash is the king of country music. He and his wife, June, are active in Christian work and, among other things, frequently appear at Billy Graham Crusades.

Q. *The pressures and temptations of show business must be enormous. As a Christian, what do you find the greatest challenge to your spiritual life and how does Satan attack you at this weak point?*

A. My challenge is no greater than that of any other Christian. Christians are called to be Christians. I don't think that any of us should expect or suspect that we have any special, unique calling from God—unless we have a vision as Paul did. And I don't have that vision. I'm called simply to be a Christian and I'm called and directed to seek out truth and understanding of the workings and the ways of the Christian life in private life as well as public—backstage as well as in the living room with my family.

Temptations are certainly there and I've experienced my share of them over the years. They're still there every day, but the thing about it is that every day is a brand new opportunity to touch people's lives. We can witness whether our world is the bus station or the stage. Every day is a new opportunity and a new obligation, if you will, to reflect Christ in one's life.

Personally, I make a daily commitment in my own heart, sometimes audibly, sometimes not. I recite certain scriptures that strengthen me. Still, I'm susceptible to what the world has to offer just like everyone else. But I make that daily commitment.

One of the verses that means a great deal to me is Psalm 19:14, "Let the words of my mouth, and the meditation of my heart, be acceptable in thy sight, O Lord, my strength and my redeemer." When I'm faced with temptation of various kinds, whether it be a 200-calorie soft drink or something else beautiful, I try to remember to recite that scripture and keep it implanted in my heart.

Q. *Do you ever get depressed?*

A. You know, people say you're not supposed to get depressed if you're a Christian and filled with joy. I have some of the deepest periods of depression that you can imagine. I must be perfectly honest about it. There are times that I want to go off in the woods and cry, because of what I feel is too big a load for me to carry in the world.

Like I said, we're only called to be Christians and I don't feel any special calling, but I seem to have been given much by God. And much seems to be required of me. There are obligations: people in my employ, my family, my friends, and then the world itself—the people who call at my office and knock on my door. I'm just a country boy, who grew up in the quiet country. The strain sometimes gets to be too much and I do have, not just fits of depression, but two- or three-day periods of long depression, deep depression, yes.

Q. *When you and June have disagreements, what do you fight about?*

A. In the first place, we don't fight. If we have a disagreement, we decide whether the thing we're disagreeing about is worth the trouble. If it's not, we drop it, each with his or her own opinion, but respecting the other.

If it's something that has to be worked out, we calmly and quietly sit down and face each other. Then we weigh it and work it out. We don't yell. In ten years of marriage, our voices have not been raised at each other in our home.

Q. *A nineteenth century poet named James Henry Lee Hunt wrote a poem on fame in which he said something about fame being like a coy woman who, when pursued, would flee from you, but if not pursued, would come to rest on the shoulder of the one not seeking her. Do you find that fame has been a mixed blessing for you—and how have you handled it in light of the scriptural admonition not to think of yourself more highly than you ought to? People are out there screaming, adoring you, asking for encores!*

A. They're having fun and I'm the object of their—whatever. The excitement, I enjoy that. But I certainly don't accept their adulation and the "oh, let me touch you" approach. That kind of thing turns me off. It embarrasses me. I'm embarrassed in public places or planes when people make a fuss over me.

Q. *It never inflates your ego? You never feel worthy of the adulation?*

A. No. I don't think any man should ever feel worthy of that kind of adulation. No, I go along with it. It's part of what I do. I'm in the entertainment business. Occasionally I expect that kind of reaction from people, but it always bothers me. Not when I'm on stage, because I'm all caught up in it then. That's what I'm trying to do. I'm talking about the real me when I'm off stage.

Q. *Many people are reluctant to speak about their faith for fear of being considered strange or weird. Do you find that it's easier because you are well known to be a good witness or do you think it would be easier if your name was John Smith and you drove a truck?*

A. I think it would be a *lot* easier if I were John Smith and drove a truck. But I don't find it difficult to talk about my faith. Whenever I'm asked I jump right into the subject and answer the questions. And I've had some unusual inquiries from different people at times!

I enjoy witnessing to my faith. When I started doing it publicly on television and in interviews I expected that my following would drop away very drastically. As it happened, it didn't. Oh, there was a drop here and there. That gave my life a chance to get back to normal. Being on television every week put me out in front of the world. I was in their living room and I was part of the family, which made me feel good. But there was a little too much demand. When I came out as a witness for the Lord, a lot of my old fans dropped away. But many of them didn't. I expected it to cost me. I expected it to cost me a lot more than it already has. Worldwise, I mean.

Q. *You talked a moment ago about going through many struggles during different periods of your life. People struggle with various problems. For some, it's ego or*

166

money. What are you struggling with now? You seem to be on top of the world. You have everything anyone could ever want . . . a beautiful wife, lovely children, fame. Some of these things people pursue all their lives.

A. As always, I'm struggling to keep some kind of sanity, some kind of calm and peace and quiet in the midst of all the turmoil. Concerts and traveling and schedules—that's always a struggle for me. To keep my peace of mind, to roll with the punches, to take things as they come—that's what I strive for. I'm also working very hard writing a story called "The Gospel Ship." It's the story of Paul the apostle. I try to work on it every day a little bit—in my room or on the plane. It's become like an obsession with me to write the story. There have been some great stories written on the apostle Paul. I've studied his life and I'm fascinated with it.

Q. *Is it a novel?*

A. I think it will be. We'll eventually do a film called "The Gospel Ship," as we did "Gospel Road."

Q. *Do you feel that God has allowed you to become what you are for a purpose and what is that purpose? Do you have a clear vision of that?*

A. Fairly clear, I think. I prayed when I began in this business twenty-three years ago for a hit gospel song. God gave me "A Boy Named Sue" instead! I kept praying for a hit gospel song and he gave me "Folsom Prison Blues." I kept praying for a gospel hit song and he gave me "Ring of Fire"!

"I'd like to be . . . a good daddy"

Q. *Don't forget "Ballad of a Teenage Queen"!*

A. "Ballad of a Teenage Queen"? See, we're coming right back to where we started. I'm called to be a witness. I'm called to be a Christian, wherever I am. Well, those records were like a beacon. They attracted a lot of people. And the appearances that followed attracted a lot of people. I think maybe if there's one person who might be touched with something we say or do as we go through a city then I might have come close to beginning to live up to my obligation.

Q. *If you could exchange places with anyone in the world for just one day and have their power or influence to right some wrong—who would you like to be?*

A. Just for one day, right?

Q. *One day.*

A. I know a 78-year-old man named Hoy Jones, who's a retired farmer. He does nothing but sit on his front porch and wave at people. I'd like to do that one day. I'd like to be Hoy Jones one day. Who was it that said, "Let me live in a house beside the road and be a friend to man"? Well, that's what I'd like to do if I only had one day. I'd take it.

Q. *One hundred years from now, how would you like to be remembered? For the hit records or for something else? What have you done in your life besides sell millions of records that you feel would be a proper monument to you?*

A. I'd like to be remembered as a good daddy.